F A

John Reumann, General Editor

Iscariot

by BERTIL GÄRTNER

translated by Victor I. Gruhn

EUG. TYSON
12 HiLTON DR C-3
WEST HAVEN CT.

FORTRESS PRESS   PHILADELPHIA

This book is a translation from the German of Bertil Gärtner's "Judas Iskariot," an essay which appeared in *Die rätselhaften Termini Nazoräer und Iskariot* (Horae Soederblomianae [Travaux publiés par la Société Nathan Söderblom], 4; Uppsala, 1957, distributed by C.W.K. Gleerup, Lund), pp. 37–68. It is translated here with the permission of the author. (A Swedish version of this essay appeared in *Svensk Exegetisk Årsbok* 21 [1956]: 50–81.)

Published by Fortress Press, 1971

Copyright © 1971 by FORTRESS PRESS

Library of Congress Catalog Card Number 73-157544

ISBN 0–8006–3065–3

2817D71   Printed in U.S.A.   1-3065

Contents

Editor's Introduction   **v**

ISCARIOT

1. Introduction   1
   Judas in the History of Interpretation   2
   The Name "Iscariot"   5

2. The "Fulfillment of Scripture" Motif   8
   "He Who Eats My Bread . . ." (Ps. 41:9) in John   8
   In Acts and Mark   11
   In Jesus' Own View   13

3. The Motif of "Greed for Money"   16
   The Anointing at Bethany and Judas's Actions   16
   The Intent of Judas (Mark 14, Matthew 26)   19

4. The "Demonology" Motif   22
   "Satan Entered In . . ." (Luke 22, John 13)   22
   Judas, a Symbolic Figure?   23
       In Luke–Acts   24
       In the Fourth Gospel   25
       The Background in Jewish Literature   27

5. Judas Typology in the New Testament   30
   Ahithophel as a Type   30
       "Betrayal"   32
       "By My Trusted Friend"   32
       The Traitor's Suicide   34
       Sorrow unto Death   35
       The Traitor's Fate   36
       The Demonic   38
   Summary   39

For Further Reading   40

Editor's Introduction

H E has gone down in history as "Judas who was guide to those who arrested Jesus" (Acts 1:16), "Judas Iscariot who betrayed him," the traitor. All four New Testament evangelists describe Judas thus or, in even worse terms, as a devil, Satan incarnate.

But what was this man really like, the son of Simon, who was "one of the twelve"? Why did be betray his master? How did he die? What shall we say of his significance? The figure of Judas has fascinated scholar and simple reader of the New Testament alike, learned theologians and bizarre sectarian groups. Many theories have resulted, about his surname "Iscariot," his motives, and the meaning of his deed "on the night in which our Lord Jesus was betrayed."

In the essay which follows, Professor—now Bishop—Bertil Gärtner, a Swedish biblical theologian who once taught at Princeton Seminary and is now in charge of the diocese of Gothenburg in the (Lutheran) Church of Sweden, assesses some of these views and places Judas squarely within the context of "salvation history." He examines the various approaches taken to Judas from New Testament times on, in light of supposed meanings of the term "Iscariot," and, rejecting the widespread theory that Judas acted out of greed for money, finds that the two motifs of scriptural fulfillment and demonology (or domination by Satan) have coalesced. Taken together, these motifs provide us with a "typological" presentation of Judas which draws on the portrayal of Old Testament traitors like

Ahithophel (who betrayed King David in 2 Samuel 16–17) in late Jewish rabbinic and Qumran literature.

Of course, even if this thesis is fully accepted, many enigmas still remain about Judas, and some readers will wish to question this detail or that point in the view which Dr. Gärtner sets forth. Nonetheless, the essay introduces us to a major line of solution for the "Judas problem" and acquaints us with a widespread kind of biblical exegesis which draws on linguistic details and verbal hints in ancient texts to weave together a typology from the ancient biblical world of thought.

As the essay makes clear, many assessments have been ventured of Judas. Donatus Haugg, a Catholic biblical scholar writing in 1930 in a doctoral dissertation on Judas (for full title and details on literature mentioned here, see the section "For Further Reading" at the end of this book), traced four main interpretations over the centuries: (1) Judas as sinner, dominated by greed (cf. the text of the Oberammergau Passion Play, as developed in 1634)—at times this interpretation took on anti-Semitic overtones, with "Judas" being equated with "the Jew" or "Jews" generally; (2) Judas as the devil incarnate, a monster of perfidy (the Fourth Gospel already tends in this direction); (3) Judas the hero, who meant his actions for good or, in the opinion of some sects in the patristic period, actually was the key figure in the redemptive drama, by bringing Jesus to fulfillment of his saving work; and (4) Judas as the object of legend—such a figure came to attract stories of all sorts, some fictional, some perhaps factual, a tendency which began already in early Christian times. To that list might be added the theory that Judas never lived but is merely a symbolic figure (so Schläger in 1914, on the "unhistoricity of the betrayer Judas" —this was a period when the historical existence of Jesus himself was questioned by some)! Wild fables abounded, especially in the Middle Ages, sometimes in connection with the "wandering Jew" legend or spread by such works as that of a seventeenth-century Vienna priest, Abraham a Santa Clara (Ulrich Megerle), translated into English as *The Arch-Knave, or the History of Judas from the Cradle to the Gallows.*

It is tempting to explore in detail some of these notions about Judas which developed in the course of the history of interpretation. Dr. Gärtner's essay alludes to certain of them. In addition to Haugg's survey and a monograph in English by Halas, there are discussions of Judas in early Christian tradition by Wrede and Walter Bauer, as well as references in the English translation of the Hennecke-Schneemelcher *New Testament Apocrypha.* Some of these treatments note church fathers like Origen and John Chrysostom who gave special attention to Judas (see especially Laeuchli's article on Origen). There are surveys on Judas in medieval legend by Creizenbach and Baum. For the period since the Reformation, a book in German by Kurt Lüthi provides thorough analysis, and there is even an older nineteenth-century treatment by Porte on Judas as portrayed in art.

One could easily go on adding examples and pointing out particular treatments of Judas, down to the present. For example, in the musical composition by William White, "The Passion According to a Cynic" (1971), the very name of Judas is hissed by the chorus when he is mentioned, "Judas-s-s." Pope Paul VI in his 1971 Maundy Thursday homily bitterly likened to Judas those priests who defect, whose "moral mediocrity" leads them to desert "for vile earthly reasons." One early nineteenth-century theologian made Judas the symbol for all evil in his discussion of good and evil (Karl Daub, *Judas Iscarioth, oder Böse in Verhältniss zum Guten* [Heidelberg; 1816–18]. On the other hand, Karl Barth has tended to give Judas a rather positive evaluation (cf. *Church Dogmatics* II/2, *The Doctrine of God* [Edinburgh: T. & T. Clark, 1957], pp. 485–506). And some commentators have even suggested that Judas was the brother of Mary, Martha, and Lazareth of Bethany (on the grounds that he was present in their home at John 12 when Jesus was anointed by Mary before his death).

The Cainites, a gnostic sect of the late second century A.D., mentioned by the church father Irenaeus about A.D. 180, hailed Judas as significant because he withstood the Demiurge or Creator God and thus must have been on the side of the Highest God whom Jesus revealed. Some Gnostics may even have revered Judas more than Jesus. Here typology seems to have run amuck in a system which celebrated "the mystery of the betrayal" and claimed a "Gospel of Judas" (A.D. 150 or so, cf. Hennecke-Schneemelcher, Vol. 1, pp. 313 f.): Iscariot was a type of the passion of Sophia, the twelfth aeon in the gnostic system, just as Judas was regularly the twelfth in the list of Jesus' disciples—"who 'betrayed' his Lord."

Another extreme interpretation of Judas is that put forth by the Jewish scholar, Joseph Klausner, in his famous book *Jesus of Nazareth*. Klausner paints Judas as a devoted disciple whose ardor for Jesus cooled as he saw how Jesus contradicted himself in his teachings, failed sometimes in attempts at healing, and sought to escape his enemies out of fear. (Klausner attributes to Judas's "train of reasoning" a series of divergencies in Jesus' teachings which can be observed by modern critics in our written gospels. He regards Judas as an educated Judean—in contrast to the other uneducated Galilean disciples—who alone saw through Jesus.) From the incident at Caesarea Philippi onward, Judas regarded Jesus as a false prophet, leading the people astray. At Jerusalem he might have hoped Jesus would reveal the power Judas had once hoped for from him, but Jesus did no miracles in the Holy City. Hence he was a fraud. Judas saw it as his duty, on the basis of Deuteronomy 13:1–11, which commanded that such false teachers who encourage rebellion against God be purged from Israel, to report Jesus to the authorities and bring him to his death.

What became of Judas is variously reported. Already in the New Testament we have two differing traditions about his death. Matthew 27:3–10 says he hanged himself. Acts 1:18–19, a parenthetical note in a speech by Peter, says Judas fell headlong (or "swelled up"—the meaning of the Greek is much debated; Thomas De Quincey once argued it was to be taken metaphorically, "plunged to utter ruin"); then Judas "burst open in the middle, and all his bowels gushed out." (De Quincey suggested that "bowels" be taken in the usual biblical, metaphorical sense, for the seat of the emotions, thus meaning Judas died "broken-hearted.") Commentators over the years have busied themselves with attempts to reconcile these two accounts, even by looking for a location at the southeast corner of the walls of Jerusalem where a tree branch, from which Judas might have hanged himself, extended over the Kidron Valley near the field of Akeldama—Judas might thus have fallen and disemboweled himself after the rope broke! (There are all sorts of other difficulties in the two accounts. Matthew seems to make Judas rue, though not repent of, his betrayal; Luke lacks that detail. The name "Akeldama" is variously explained as "field of blood"— because it was purchased with blood-money from Jesus' betrayal [Matthew 27:6], or because the blood of Judas was poured out on it [cf. Acts 1:19]; in Acts, Judas purchases that field, in Matthew the priests purchase it with the blood-money which Judas had returned. We simply do not know the full details of how Judas died.)

Complicating matters still more and reflecting the way stories multiplied about Judas, there is a third tradition concerning the fate of Judas. It quotes from the *Exegesis of the Dominical Oracles* by Papias of Hierapolis about A.D. 130, as preserved in one Apollinarius of Laodicea (bishop and heresiologist in the fourth century), extant in two different catena or "chains" of patristic traditions on Acts 1 and Matthew 27. In essence harmonizing Matthew and Acts, Apollinarius says Judas did not die by hanging but was taken down before he choked to death and lived on until he later met the death described in Acts. To support this point, Papias is quoted:

Judas went about a great example of impiety in this world. His flesh was swollen to such an extent that he could not get through a place where a wagon might easily go through! Not even his bulky head could get through by itself! They say his eyelids were so swelled that he could not see the light at all; his eyes could not be seen by a physician with an optical instrument, to such a depth had they sunk from the outward surface. His private part appeared more huge and loathsome than any man's "shame." Through it he passed pus and worms flowing together from every part of his body, to his shame, when he relieved himself. After many torments and punishments he died, they say, on his own piece of land [some render: went to the place where he belonged]. Because of the stench this place has become deserted and uninhabited till the present. Down to today no one can pass by that spot unless he covers his nose with his hands—to such an extent has the discharge progressed through his flesh and over the ground.

Surely here the hatred for the arch-villain is apparent. Even though Judas outlived his suicide attempt and perhaps even enjoyed some of his ill-gotten gains, monstrous suffering was visited upon him, in life and after death.

There are also modern speculations about Judas. One writer, for example, Albert Lévitt, unconvinced by what he learned of Judas in theological school, has composed Judas's "autobiography," as the son of the high priest in the temple (!) in Kerioth might have written it. Here Judas emerges as Jesus' most reliable disciple, entrusted with revealing to the hierarchy Jesus' real identity as Messiah. He was such a man that the contradictory accounts of his death in early Christianity could not have been true; he must have died by his own hand in order to be with Jesus. There are also frankly fictional retellings of the biblical accounts, like that by A. and E. Van Heurn, where Judas acts to save Jesus by seeking to have him make peace with his crafty enemies, a ploy which ends in both the death of Jesus and the suicide of his would-be savior. There are sermons like the one by Leslie Weatherhead depicting Judas as a bit psychotic—not a puppet in a plan of God, nor a wicked demon, nor a greedy man—but a lonely Judean nationalist who believed in Jesus' heavenly power and wanted to force his hand, to call those twelve legions of angels to his aid.

We might especially observe how in some of these ancient accounts—and in the opinion of modern commentators—data from stories about the fate of classic villains in Jewish history or folklore have been used in telling of Judas. One possible analogue is the account of the death of Antiochus Epiphanes, the Seleucid king against whom the Maccabees had rebelled, in 2 Maccabees 9. When that king resolved to "make Jerusalem a cemetery of Jews," God "struck him an incurable and unseen blow" (v. 5, a heart attack?). There was "pain in his bowels," without relief (v. 5). In addition, Antiochus fell out of his chariot and was tortured in "every limb of his body" (v.

7). His body swarms with worms, his flesh rots away, and the stench nauseates his entire army, so that no one can even carry his litter (v. 9)! Deathbed repentance avails nothing, and Antiochus dies with the same intense suffering he had inflicted on others (v. 28). The death of Herod Agrippa at Acts 12:23 should be compared, and especially that of Herod the Great in Josephus, *Antiquities* 17. 168–79 (17.6.5) with its similar details (bowels, gangrene, worms). Another story compared particularly with the Acts version of the death of Judas is that of how Nadan betrayed his uncle Ahikar and, as his fate, swelled up, burst, and died, the Arabic version adding that "his entrails were scattered" and "he went to hell" (R. H. Charles, *The Apocrypha and Pseudepigrapha of the Old Testament* [Oxford: Clarendon, 1913, reprinted 1963], Vol. 2, p. 776).

Dr. Gärtner is mindful of such accounts and possible influence upon even the New Testament portrayals of the fate of Judas from them. But he chooses to see the influence as coming instead from Old Testament examples, particularly the traitor in David's life, Ahithophel, as that account was developed in rabbinic tradition. (As an aid in checking in context Dr. Gärtner's references to the Babylonian or Palestinian [Jerusalem] Talmud and to the Midrash Rabba—a collection of expository comments on the books of the Pentateuch and the "Five Scrolls" such as the Song of Solomon and Ecclesiastes, dated in the fifth and following centuries of the Christian era—reference has been added in the notes to the standard English versions edited, respectively, by Epstein and by Freedman and Simon.)

One might note too the sort of debate which has occupied some minds over the centuries, as to whether Judas, at the Last Supper, received "Holy Communion" or not. This became a dogmatic question of some importance: could a man, after receiving the sacrament, commit so heinous a crime? All four gospels state that Judas was in the Upper Room for the meal. In the Synoptics he dips bread into the same dish with Jesus and the others. In John he receives the sop or morsel of bread from Jesus before going off to his night rendezvous with the chief priests. But did he receive—could he have partaken of—the special bread and wine? There has been a considerable literature on the subject of "Judas-communion."

Such topics, conjectures, theories, and questions might be multiplied, almost indefinitely. It may be of interest for the general reader to compare with Dr. Gärtner's findings the conclusions of another investigator, Kurt Lüthi, who published in 1955 a study on Judas in the interpretation of the last four hundred years and proposed seven theses on the "Judas problem" in an article in *Evangelische Theologie* the same year that the essay in this Facet Book appeared. After examination of the New Testament references Lüthi set forth the following points:

(1) Iscariot is to be seen within the framework of "Galilee and Jerusalem." As "man of Kerioth" (geographically) he represents (in theological geography) within the disciple band that which sent Jesus to the cross.

(2) The motif of money in Judas's betrayal is not to be understood moralistically but demonologically and eschatologically.

(3) As for the age-old question of whether Judas partook of the Last Supper with Jesus, the evangelists vary in their answers. Luke seems to say he did partake; does Matthew imply Judas was excluded from the gifts of the meal?

(4) The use of the Old Testament at Mark 14:18 (". . . one of you will betray me, *one who is eating with me,*" Psalm 41:9) and at John 13:18 ("that the scripture might be fulfilled, '*He who ate my bread has lifted up his heel against me,*'" Psalm 41:9), where the "enemy" in the psalm suggests lurking "powers of chaos," points to a demonological background for the Judas references.

(5) There are different tendencies in the evangelists: Matthew is negative toward Judas, Luke more positive. Luke omits the Psalm 41:9 citation; he tones down the scene at Mark 14:18–21 where the disciples each assert their innocence by asking "It isn't I, is it?" and where—instead of words about how it would be better for the betrayer not to have been born—Luke has simply a more indefinite "woe" to that man. Matthew's very specific statement (26:25) where Jesus tells Judas he is the one, is missing in Luke. Luke neglects to say that Judas actually delivered

his traitor's kiss. And Luke lacks an account of Judas's suicide such as Matthew 27:3–10 provides. (It will be remembered that Acts has a different account of the end of this disciple, 1:18 f.) When we recall that Luke also seems to allow that Judas partook of the meal—and thus of the atoning power of the death of Jesus, the new covenant, and the eschatological hope—then perhaps Lüthi is correct in conjecturing that the treatment of Judas here corresponds to a christological emphasis: Luke's universalism (the Gospel for *all* men) is here reflected, a Lord who prays, "Father, forgive them . . ." (Luke 23:34)—even Judas?

(6) John portrays Judas as an unbeliever who takes part in the meal, a devil who represents the power of Satan and the Antichrist, an incarnation of the forces of chaos.

(7) Yet for all this negative portrayal, going far beyond the Synoptics in blackening the picture of Judas, John also, as part of his presentation, sees these powers of chaos as powerless before Christ. The cross is a revelation of his glory. And Judas? There is no account of a gruesome end. He is left standing there with the opponents (18:5). He who went out into the night (13:30) simply vanishes into nothingness, where he belongs.

These suggestions, when placed alongside Dr. Gärtner's work, the result of a totally independent study, help to establish as proper the emphasis Gärtner places on the twin motifs of fulfillment of Scripture and the demonological.

The author of our study on Judas was born in Gothenburg, Sweden, in 1924. After theological studies at Uppsala, Bertil E. Gärtner was ordained in the Church of Sweden in 1948 and had pastoral duties for three years. He received his doctorate in 1955 for a study on Acts 17, published (in English translation) as *The Areopagus Speech and Natural Revelation* (1955). In that monograph Dr. Gärtner argued that Luke's historical writing is best compared not so much with Greek historians as with Jewish writers (1, 2 Maccabees, Josephus) and that Luke may be said to have had good sources at his disposal. Accordingly, the speech attributed to Paul before the Areopagus is not to be judged a later insertion based on concepts from Stoic natural revelation, but a speech Pauline in character, reflecting Old Testament and late Jewish concepts, though its form may show Lukan influence.

For Dr. Gärtner appointment followed to the faculty at Uppsala, as docent or assistant professor of New Testament, 1955–64, and associate professor of Old Testament, 1964–65. In 1965 he accepted a chair in New Testament at Princeton Theological Seminary, where he taught until returning to Sweden in late 1969 to become Dean of Gothenburg Cathedral and then in 1970 bishop of the diocese as successor of Bo Giertz.

Over the years Professor Gärtner has written a number of books and articles, in Swedish, German, and English (see "For Further Reading"), especially in the *Svensk Exegetisk Årsbok,* for which he was editorial secretary 1953–59, and the *Svensk Bibliskt Uppslags Verk* (1962–63), an encyclopedia to which he contributed some forty articles. Major works include a study of John 6 and the Jewish Passover; the Gospel of Thomas; "temple" imagery in the Dead Sea Scrolls and the New Testament; and commentaries in Swedish on Mark (1967) and the Johannine epistles (1969). His interests as a churchman are reflected in papers prepared for the Lutheran–Roman Catholic dialogue in the United States and for the Lutheran World Federation's study project on "True Humanity and the Lordship of Christ."

The translation for the Facet Books edition has been made at the author's request from the German version (1957), to which a Swedish version (dated 1956) also makes reference. The translator, the Reverend Victor I. Gruhn, Ph.D.,, is pastor of the Lutheran Church of the Resurrection, Maple Glen, Pennsylvania. He has previously taught Old Testament at the Lutheran Seminary, Philadelphia, and is known for his translations of Martin Noth's *The Old Testament World* (1966) and Gerd Wilk's *Journeys with Jesus and Paul* (1970). He has also edited the English version of Heinrich Bornkamm's *Luther and the Old Testament* (1969).

Expansion of the footnotes, insertion of chapter and sub-headings, etc., are the editor's responsibility.

Something ought to be said, finally, about the fact that the essay here translated appears in its German version with another essay by Dr. Gärtner on "Nazareth, 'Nazarene,' and Mandean-ism", under the general title, "Two Enigmatic Terms, 'Naza-rene' and 'Iscariot.' " It will be noted in the study about Judas that a decision on the derivation and significance of the word "Iscariot" is crucial, and Gärtner differs from Lüthi on what he makes of this term. (Dr. Gärtner's German essay even employs the spelling "Iskariot" instead of the more common "Ischari-oth" because of the derivation he follows; we have kept in Eng-lish the usual form as satisfactory for the linguistic point he makes in his introductory chapter.) The other essay also centers on word derivation and its theological significance. Since the Judas essay once alludes to this study on "Nazarene," a brief summary of the companion study follows.

The widely acknowledged problems in the New Testament references to Jesus as a "Nazarene" and specifically in Matthew 2:23—Jesus "went and dwelt in a city called Nazareth, that what was spoken by the prophets might be fulfilled, 'He shall be called a Nazarene' "—are not merely debate over Nazareth as a place (a Hebrew inscription mentioning it has now turned up) but (1) the two New Testament spellings of the term (*Nazōraios, Nazarēnos*) and hence its derivation, and (2) the Old Testament source which Matthew has in mind. Frequently Isaiah 11:1 and verses like it are presumed, which refer to a *nēṣer,* "branch" or "sprout" (of David). Others have proposed the Hebrew term *nāzir,* "Nazirite," as at Judges 13:5 (and 16:17), where Samson is described as a "Nazirite to God." In these cases Jesus is either a "New David" or a "New Samson," typologically. Others assume a pre-Christian Jewish sect called the "observants" or "devotees," i.e., those who observe the com-mandments, employing the Hebrew root *nṣr;* hence, *Nasaraioi* or *Nazōraioi* in Greek, a name applied to Christians, leading in turn to the notion that Jesus was "from Nazareth." Cf. Oscar

Cullmann, "Nazarene," in *The Interpreter's Dictionary of the Bible* (New York and Nashville: Abingdon, 1962), Vol. 3, pp. 523 f.

Dr. Gärtner, after sketching the facts and finding a number of previous solutions not completely satisfying, argues that in Matthew 1–2, built as the chapters are around the terms "Emmanuel," "king of the Jews," and *Nazōraios,* we have an Old Testament term applied to Jesus. It comes from the root meaning "observe" or "keep" but should be interpreted as a passive participle, *nāṣûr,* "that which is kept, guarded, or preserved" by God, i.e., reflecting the "holy remnant" (cf. Isaiah 42:6 ff.; 49:6, 8; 60:21; and also 11:1) and above all Qumran Thanksgiving Hymns like 1QH 8.6 ff. (about a "shoot") and Mandean references to "observants." Jesus would thus be the one "kept" for his messianic task, his followers the "holy remnant, those kept." (Gärtner alludes to this interpretation in his monograph on *Temple and the Community,* pp. 132 f.)

This explanation must remain uncertain in the present state of scholarship, for some exegetes have rejected it in favor of other understandings of "Nazarene" (cf. Cullmann). Eduard Schweizer, *The Good News According to Mark,* tr. by Donald H. Madvig (Richmond: John Knox, 1970), p. 52, drawing on his earlier article in the Jeremias festschrift (*Judentum, Urchristentum, Kirche* [Berlin: Töpelmann, 1960], pp. 90–93), prefers the Nazirite explanation, but calls attention to how at Judges 16:17 there are two different Greek manuscript traditions: one calls Samson a *naz(e)iraios,* the other "God's holy one." On this explanation, reflecting both variants, Jesus would have been identified by the early church as a "New Samson," the "holy one of God," a Nazirite/Nazarene, from Nazareth. J. A. Sanders has developed this Samson parallel further in an article in the *Journal of Biblical Literature* 84 (1965): 169–72.

In each instance Dr. Gärtner has presented us with what may be termed a typological approach. Space does not permit discussion of "typology" as a method for employing the Scriptures, either in early Christianity or today, though a few titles from recent discussion have been included in the bibliography "For

Further Reading." Opinions vary and even the definition of what "types" and "antitypes" involve, but the method has long had, and still attracts, a considerable following.

C. K. Barrett, in his review of these twin essays (in *The Journal of Theological Studies* N.S. 11 [1960]: 135 f.), expressed the hope that Dr. Gärtner would go on and further develop the "interesting and instructive" typological interpretation which he found applied to Psalm 41 and other Old Testament passages in early Christianity, since "a creative understanding of the Old Testament was one of the factors that produced the New Testament and its theology." Some of Bishop Gärtner's other writings assume, or reflect, the approach used here, and this essay is presented to exemplify the method which these pages have sought to introduce.

JOHN REUMANN

Lutheran Theological Seminary
Philadelphia
April, 1971

1

INTRODUCTION

J UDAS Iscariot is a fascinating figure in New Testament study and, because of his fate, has given rise to much speculation about himself. The fact that he betrayed Jesus into the hands of his enemies has sometimes been treated as an inhuman crime, a loathsome and contemptuous deed. Then again, the role which he plays in the gospels has been described sympathetically, and attempts have been made to defend or even excuse him, for one reason or another.[1]

Within the New Testament canon, interest in the figure of Judas is not so great. A reading of the New Testament gives rather the impression that the traditions about Judas might have been suppressed in primitive Christianity. The action of Judas must have been an embarrassment to Christians; about him no edifying reference could be handed down. What the record needed was simply the fact that it was Judas who took the astounding step of betraying Jesus, and something about the manner in which Jesus fell into the hands of his enemies. Beyond this, there entered in indirectly some of the questions and opinions with which the primitive church was troubled regarding the cause for that puzzling act, namely, that one of the twelve apostles could deal thus with the Messiah.

1. See Kurt Lüthi, *Judas Iskarioth in der Geschichte der Auslegung von der Reformation bis in die Gegenwart* (Zürich: Zwingli Verlag, 1955). p. 75, and Gert Buchheit, *Judas Iskarioth: Legende, Geschichte, Deutung* (Gütersloh: Rufer-Verlag, 1954).

JUDAS IN THE HISTORY OF INTERPRETATION

Among the Apostolic Fathers we find nothing about Judas except for a brief reference in the *Shepherd of Hermas* and a legendary account about the manner of the death of Judas in a fragment of Papias.[2] On the other hand, we find a greater interest in the figure of Judas in patristic literature. This developed in part in the dogmatic controversies of the ancient church. Above all, Origen treated the story of Judas in detail, in order to confront the mockers and critics of Christian faith. At the same time he directed himself against those within the church who taught that Judas was predestined from birth to be lost. Origen thereby defended the thesis that Judas was at first a good, believing man, just like the other apostles—no worse than Peter, a friend of Jesus and a man with free will. Within the circle of Jesus Judas even held the responsible office of treasurer.[3] Origen sees the reason for the betrayal in Judas's lack of faith and his love for money.[4] Judas could not exercise self-control, and therefore his love of money won out.

2. *Hermas,* Similitude 8.6.4: "Those whose rods proved to be withered and worm-eaten are the apostates and betrayers of the church who have blasphemed the Lord by their sins and also have brought shame to the Name of the Lord which was invoked over them. These therefore have been lost to God forever." See also 9.19.1.

Papias, Fragment III (in *Patrum Apostolicorum Opera,* ed. by O. Gebhardt, A. Harnack, and T. Zahn [Leipzig: Hinrichs, 1906], p. 73), is preserved by Apollinaris. See Donatus Haugg, *Judas Iskarioth in den neutestamentlichen Berichten* (Freiburg: Herder, 1930), pp. 39 ff.

In this connection some statements from the *Martyrdom of Polycarp,* section 6, should be mentioned, where Judas is presented as the prototype of all betrayers among Christians. "And when they did not find him [Polycarp], they seized two young slaves. one of whom confessed under torture. It was impossible that Polycarp should remain hidden, since those who betrayed him were from his own household. The police chief, who was named Herod—the very name!—hastened to bring him [Polycarp] to the stadium so that he could fulfill his particular calling, by becoming a partner with Christ, while his betrayers received the punishment of Judas." See P. A. van Stempvoort, *Waarheid en verbeelding rondom het Nieuwe Testament* (1956), pp. 97 ff., on the apocryphal literature; also E. Hennecke, *New Testament Apocrypha,* ed. by W. Schneemelcher, tr. by R. McL. Wilson *et al.* (Philadelphia: Westminster), Vol. 1 (1963). pp. 505–507 (Gospel of Bartholomew); Vol. 2 (1965), pp. 62 f., 290 (Acts of Peter), 460 and 487 (Acts of Thomas).

3. Haugg (cited above, n. 2), pp. 22 f.

4. S. Laeuchli, "Origen's Interpretation of Judas Iscariot," *Church History* 22 (1953): 254, cf. 257.

Certain gnostic trends also forced interest in the figure of Judas. These Gnostics revered Judas almost as a divine being. Among those whom Irenaeus calls Cainites, Judas figured as the first Gnostic. They said this because he was the only person in the gospels who recognized the truth in the person of Jesus—by his betrayal, Judas precipitated separation of the heavenly from the earthly.[5] This positive interest in Judas develops in the following period into medieval Jewish legends about Judas. In these he is defended against the Christian judgment on him as the betrayer, a defense which grew out of the persecutions of the Jews in that period.[6]

The most dominant concept of Judas was, and is, that which sees him as a man ruled by greed for money, who sold Jesus to gain money. This view already marks completely, for example, the interpretation of the betrayer by John Chrysostom. It is still the most popular, even if in exegetical literature of more recent date other motives have been ascribed, such as lack of faith, a false understanding of messiahship, or possession by Satan.[7] A support for this understanding of Judas as a greedy person is provided by clear statements in the Johannine pericope about the anointing of Jesus at Bethany (John 12:1–11). There Judas saw a waste in pouring out that costly nard; in his protest he stated that the money—three hundred denarii [about one year's pay for a laborer]—should rather have been given to the poor. John comments on that reaction of Judas with these words: "He

5. Irenaeus, *Against Heresies* (*Adv. haeres.*) 1.31.1, "Others, again, regard Cain as descended from the Power on high. They account Esau, Korah, the Sodomites, and the like as their relatives, who were hated by their Creator, though they suffered nothing worse from him. For Wisdom (Sophia) took to herself from them what belonged to her. Of that the betrayer, Judas, was well aware. He alone knew the truth and accomplished the mystery of the betrayal. He separated everything earthly and heavenly. This fiction they call the Gospel of Judas." See Haugg (cited above, n. 2), pp. 47 f.
6. See S. Krauss, *Das Leben Jesu nach jüdischen Quellen* (Berlin, 1902), p. 176; B. Heller, "Über Judas Ischariotes in der jüdischen Legende," *Monatsschrift für Geschichte und Wissenschaft des Judentums* 76 (1932): 33–42.
7. See Haugg (cited above, n. 2), pp. 105 ff.; Roman Bernard Halas, *Judas Iscariot. A Scriptural and Theological Study of his Person, his Deeds and his Eternal Lot* (Studies in Sacred Theology, 96 [Washington, D.C.: The Catholic University of America Press, 1946]), pp. 79 ff.; Lüthi, *Judas Iskarioth* (cited above, n. 1), pp. 155 ff.

said this, not because he cared about the poor, but because he was a thief and as holder of the common fund helped himself to the money" (John 12:6). We read further of Judas's love for money at Matthew 26:14 f., "Then one of the twelve named Judas Iscariot went to the chief priests and said: 'What do you want to give to me, if I should betray him to you?' Then they weighed out for him (placed before him) thirty silver pieces."

On occasion, predominantly moralistic aspects have been applied to the money motif. It has been asserted that in all of the pericopes about Judas there lies a parenetic tone: the Judas narratives served to censure greed, a censure which is common, moreover, in Jewish parenetic writings, especially in the intertestamental literature. This moralistic view has now been replaced by an understanding that proceeds from the obvious connection between *adikia* [wickedness] and money in the New Testament. A certain demonological connection thereby comes into view which provides an important trait in the presentation of Judas.[8] This is also related to the question which is seen as early as Origen, namely, what place Judas holds in the fulfillment of salvation history.[9] At the least, Judas appears to be a significant figure in realization of the divine plans of salvation. John's Gospel especially states clearly that Jesus knew from the beginning of the betrayal, and that this betrayal was predicted in Scripture. Satan, in his fight against Jesus, makes a pact with Judas—it is stated of Judas himself that he is a *diabolos*—and it is Satan's proposition to which Judas makes himself subservient. One should view as in accord with that a reference to Psalm 41:9 at John 13:18. Here John seeks to portray Judas's betrayal as a battle between God and the powers of chaos: the "enemy" —that is, according to Old Testament concepts, the power which is hostile to God and breaks covenant—takes shape in Judas, and he becomes the "representative of the counter force."[10]

8. K. Lüthi, "Das Problem des Judas Iskariot—neu untersucht," *Evangelische Theologie* 16 (1956): 99 f.
9. Laeuchli (cited above, n. 4), pp. 264 f.
10. Lüthi, "Das Problem des Judas Iskariot" (cited above, n. 8), pp. 102 f.

These are very noteworthy points of view, which open new and deeper perspectives on Judas and his deed. However, in spite of the fact that the problems surrounding Judas have been the object of extended research, it seems to me that there are still points which are unclear, as there probably always will be. The essay which follows seeks merely to point out some aspects with reference to the place which Judas occupies in primitive Christian theology.

THE NAME "ISCARIOT"

The surname "Iscariot" is a good place to begin a discussion about the figure of Judas. "Iscariot" is obviously a hellenized form of one or more Semitic words. The difficulty lies in finding the proper background for the word formation. The most important attempts to find the meaning which were previously undertaken, do not need to be repeated here, since there are good surveys of these.[11]

The most common meaning given again and again in the literature is "Iscariot"="man of Kerioth," or *'ish q^eriyyôth*. This derives from the Judean town mentioned in Joshua 15:25, Jeremiah 48:24, and elsewhere. Judas's origin from Judea was accordingly understood to have produced an antagonism, even from the beginning, between Judas and the other disciples, who came from Galilee. In this manner Judas was linked with Jerusalem, where the dramatic events surrounding the death of Jesus took place.[12] However, the American philologian Charles C. Torrey, in his noteworthy article on the meaning of the name Iscariot, has now demonstrated that that meaning suffers from so many deficiencies that it can be considered impossible. One

11. See, e.g., Charles C. Torrey, "The Name 'Iscariot,'" *Harvard Theological Review* 36 (1943): 51–62; Halas (cited above, n. 7), pp. 11 f.; Harald Ingholt, "The Surname of Judas Iscariot," in *Studia orientalia Ioanni Pedersen . . . dicata* (Copenhagen: Munksgaard, 1953), pp. 155–58.
12. Thus Haugg (cited above, n. 2), pp. 76 ff.; Lüthi, "Das Problem des Judas Iskariot" (cited above, n. 8), p. 99, ". . . opinion has mostly remained with the old consensus: Judas is the man from Kerioth, a village in Judea . . . likewise, it is true that Judas has this surname to avoid confusing him with another disciple with the same name, and that the surname already belonged to his family (John 6:71)."

needs to think only of the difficulties that result if one looks for the existence of a town called Kerioth, or of the problems which result from using the Hebrew word *'ish* (man) as part of a name which was developed in an Aramaic-speaking milieu.[13]

Another explanation for "Iscariot" which still appears in the literature is derivation of the name from the Greek word *sikarios*, which means "bandit," "assassin," "cut-throat."[14] Torrey shows that this meaning is completely untenable: both in the Latin form *sicarius* and in the Greek *sikarios* the *i* in the first syllable is long and could not have disappeared in Iscariot.[15]

The only plausible way to arrive at a meaning for the name Iscariot seems to be the one which Torrey took.[16] He attempted to reproduce the Aramaic word concealed behind this name. It should be noted then that the surname Iscariot does not have to

13. Torrey (cited above, n. 11), pp. 52–56. Torrey takes a very critical view of Gustaf Dalman, *The Words of Jesus,* tr. by D. M. Kay (Edinburgh: T. & T. Clark, 1902), pp. 51 f., where it is asserted that the Hebrew word *'ish* in the Talmud and midrash usually refers to "a man from" one town or another. "Dalman's examples and his inference from them have been very widely quoted and influential, but how this material can bear on our question is not apparent. Judas was not given his nickname by the Tannaite schoolmen, and it is *only* from their learned language that the illustrations are taken" (Torrey, p. 54). Compare Julius Wellhausen, *Das Evangelium Marci* (Berlin: Georg Reimer, 1903), p. 25, and A. Schlatter, *Der Evangelist Matthäus* (Stuttgart: Calwer, 1929), p. 327, who raised objections similar to those of Torrey.

14. Recently Oscar Cullmann has advocated this viewpoint; cf. *The State in the New Testament* (New York: Scribner's, 1956), pp. 15 f.

15. Torrey (cited above, n. 11), pp. 57 f.

16. Ingholt (cited above, n. 11), pp. 158–61, is of the opinion that the surname Iscariot can be derived from the Aramaic root *sqr,* Arabic *shqr.* This root means "be of brown color, have a ruddy complexion." "The name *Seqârai-Isqârai* 'of ruddy complexion' belongs to a well-known category of Semitic proper names. It was not a name given to Judas only after his fatal act of betrayal, but it had distinguished him from others of the same name, already before he became a disciple of Jesus" (p. 161). This explanation does not seem so convincing to me, and it does not mesh well with what the New Testament texts express.

In this connection one can refer to F. Rundgren's exposition, which links the color red with the meaning "red" in the name Esau. This "red" Esau is linked in Jewish traditions with the despised Romans. Cf. *"Sillagdun = al-aḥāmira = al-Rūm* nebst einigen Bemerkungen zu *Ibn al-Sirâfîs Šarḥ abyât Islâḥ al-mantiq,"* in *Donum natalicium H. S. Nyberg oblatam,* ed. by Erik Gren *et al.* (Uppsala, 1954), p. 143. See also Louis Ginzberg, *The Legends of the Jews* (Philadelphia: The Jewish Publication Society of America), Vol. 5 (1925), pp. 272 f., 309, 311 f.; Vol. 6 (1928), pp. 259 f.

have anything to do with Judas's hometown, but very probably was attached to him after Jesus' death. If one works out the radicals in Iscariot (*sh-q-r*), he arrives at the Aramaic *sh^eqar* or *shiqrā'* with the meaning "deceit," "fraud," "falsehood." The adjective *shiqrai, sh^eqaryā'* is also used substantively, to indicate someone who is characterized by fraud and falsehood. The specific form, "the false one," was generally given as *'ishqaryā'* with prosthetic *aleph*.[17] After Judas's betrayal became known— so runs Torrey's thesis—the form *Yehudah sheqaryā'* was developed, precisely as a term of abuse, a name which then stuck. In Greek texts *'ishqaryā'* was not translated because this form was so closely linked with Judas. Rather, the Greek denominative ending was attached, by which a noun ending in *-ia* is completed by the ending *-ōtēs*: e.g., *stratia — stratiōtēs*. The surname of Judas was treated in an analogous way: *iskaria — iskariōtēs*. This derivation seems to me to rest on good philological foundation and to have every advantage on its side.[18]

17. Charles C. Torrey, "Studies in the Aramaic of the First Century A.D.," *Zeitschrift für die alttestamentliche Wissenschaft* 65 (1953): 246 f.
18. On the question of how the words *Ioudas Simōnos Iskariōtēs,* together with the variant *Ioudas Simōnos Iskariōtou* at John 6:71 and 13:26, are to be understood, see Ingholt (cited above, n. 11), pp. 152–55. Ingholt underscores the view of Torrey, that Iscariot belongs with "Judas" and not with "Simon." The variant could be a false way of writing it. "In this presupposed Aramaic text [the original text of the Gospel] 'Judas Iscariot, son of Simon' would appear as *Judas son of Simon Iscariot,* the surname in Aramaic referring not to Simon, but to Judas. A Greek translator might easily have mistranslated these words, as he evidently did in 6.71 and 13.26."

2

THE "FULFILLMENT OF SCRIPTURE" MOTIF

THERE are certain possibilities for approaching the figure of Judas from other points of view and thus for confirming to some extent the explanation given above for the surname Iscariot as the most probable one. At the same time we can succeed in placing Judas in a definite history-of-salvation context.

"HE WHO EATS MY BREAD . . ." (PS. 41:9) IN JOHN

In John 13 there is described how Jesus on his last night washed the feet of the disciples. John's Gospel attaches to this action a longer commentary on the part of Jesus, in which Jesus indicates what role Judas is to play in the dramatic final phase. He says that the disciples are "clean," all (13:10 f.) except Judas. The eleven, when they are sent out into the world, are to represent Christ; but not the twelfth, Judas. "I do not speak of all of you; I know whom I have chosen; but (this is so,) that the scripture might be fulfilled: he who eats my bread has lifted his heel against me" (13:18). The Old Testament citation is taken from Psalm 41:9.[19] The reproduction of the psalm text in John's Gospel does not correspond to any of the known Septuagint manuscripts. It is hard to tell to what extent John cites freely or transmits a direct translation of the Hebrew text.[20]

19. Hebrew 41:10, *'ôkēl laḥmi higdil 'ālai 'āqēb.*
Greek Septuagint, *ho esthiōn artous mou emegalunen ep' eme pternismon.*
John 13, *ho trōgōn mou (or met' emou) ton arton epēren ep' eme tēn pternan autou.*
20. See C. K. Barrett, *The Gospel According to St John* (London: SPCK, 1955), pp. 370 f.

Still, John's rendition contains no deviations in content from the Hebrew text. The psalm words "He who eats my bread," can, in their setting in the text of John, be an allusion to the fact that Judas sat at the Passover meal and then went away to carry out the betrayal. However, they can also be, in accord with Jewish patterns, a metaphor for "he who receives teaching from me," "he who receives a part in my instruction." From the perspective of the further narrative in John 13, the first meaning seems, however, to have the preference. That reference to Psalm 41:9 is of unusual importance for understanding the figure of Judas. The sense of the psalm expressions, "ate my bread" and "lifted his heel against me," is not altogether clear, but the first expression seems to me to be a parallel to the preceding *'ish shalom,* in 41:9 [R.S.V., "my bosom friend," literally "a man of peace"], i.e., a man with whom he stood in a harmonious and unbroken relationship.[21] The latter expression, "lifted his heel against me," probably means: "he conspired against me."

However, what we are particularly interested in here is the use of the word *'aqēb,* "heel." There is also a verb with the same radicals, *'āqab,* which means "defraud." Both the rabbinic literature and the Qumran texts make rather common use of the double meaning of certain word stems to build up a double meaning from them. The device is also not unknown in the New Testament.[22] In John 13:18/Psalm 41:9 we have an example of this. First the meaning "heel" comes under consideration. Then the meaning "defraud" or "defrauder" resounds. From this could come a confirmation for the translation of Iscariot as "he who defrauds." At the same time one has an outstanding illustration of how well the passage cited from the Psalms fits into the narrative about Judas, ". . . that the scripture might be fulfilled." That play on words which rings behind John 13:18 is not new. It occurs also in Genesis: as Jacob was

---

21. H. Ringgren, *The Faith of the Psalmists* (Philadelphia: Fortress, 1963), p. 117.
22. Cf. B. Gärtner, "Nazareth, Nazoräer und das Mandäertum," in *Die rätselhaften Termini Nazoräer und Iskariot* (Horae Soederblomianae, 4 [Uppsala, 1957], distributed by C.W.K. Gleerup, Lund), p. 24.

born, he held on tight to Esau's heel; from this he received his name Jacob, "he who holds on tight to the heel," Genesis 25:26. In Genesis 27:36 there is a play on another meaning in the same name, "he who defrauds"; "he is properly called Jacob," says Esau, "for he has now deceived me twice."[23]

It is not only the short citation from Psalm 41 which determines the meaning for the usage in John 13. As so often elsewhere, there is, moreover, in the citation, reference to a larger portion of the Old Testament text.[24] In this case there are so many lines of connection between the entire Psalm and the Judas narrative that one dare not lose sight of these, if he wants to understand the expression ". . . that the scripture might be fulfilled." Thus we read in Psalm 41:5 (Hebrew, 41:6): "My enemies say of me in malice, 'When will he die, and his name perish?' " The content of the Psalm fits well with the situation portrayed by the evangelist on the last night before the death of Jesus, when the urgent craving of his enemies to get him out of the way seemed about to be realized. Verse 6 (Hebrew, 41:7) has: "When one comes to visit me, he speaks falsehood; his heart gathers mischief. When he goes out, he tells it abroad." This is an excellent illustration of the situation in John 13. For this is the very moment when Judas, sitting at the table, is ready to go off to Jesus' enemies to complete the betrayal and put Jesus out of the way.[25] Then the Psalm continues (vv. 7–8; Hebrew, vv. 8–9): "All who hate me whisper together about me, they imagine the worst for me. They say, 'A deadly thing has fastened upon him; he will not rise again from where he lies.' " Once more an amazingly similar application of the statements of the Psalm to the Judas narrative is produced. This application

23. See Frithiof Rundgren, *Über Bildungen mit š und n-t-Demonstrativen in Semitischen* (Beiträge zur vergleichenden Grammatik der semitischen Sprachen [Uppsala: Almqvist & Wiksells, 1955]), pp. 136 f.

24. Cf., e.g., C. H. Dodd, *According to the Scriptures: The Sub-structure of New Testament Theology* (London: Nisbet, 1952, and New York: Scribner's, 1953), p. 126.

25. The Targum of Psalm 41:6 (Hebrew, v. 7), the Aramaic rendition, has here exactly the term *sheqar*, "falsehood, fraud," which underlies the surname Iscariot. The Hebrew text here uses the word *shāw'*, "vain, empty," as reflected in the R.S.V. translation: "empty words."

culminates finally in verse 9 (Hebrew, v. 10): "Yes, even my friend (literally "the man of my peace") in whom I trusted, who ate my bread, lifted his heel against me (defrauded me)." From this, one can see how well the central part of the Psalm belongs in this situation and fits in under the formula ". . . that the scripture might be fulfilled."

What we have in the reference to Psalm 41 at John 13:18 is not only an expression of Johannine scriptural interpretation. Rather, we have reason to maintain that the early church generally regarded the betrayal by Judas under the aspect of fulfillment of Scripture, and hence treated Psalm 41 as a prophetic text. This conclusion emerges from two other texts in which we find reference to this fact.

In Acts and Mark

In Acts 1:15 ff. there is an account of how Peter proposed to the rest of the brothers that the place of Judas in the circle of the twelve should be filled by another of the disciples of Jesus. "Brothers, the scripture had to be fulfilled, which the Holy Spirit spoke beforehand by the mouth of David, concerning Judas who was guide to those who arrested Jesus. For he was numbered among us and was allotted his share in the ministry" (1:16). The reference here is to "David's Psalms" without giving a citation. What the Scriptures are here said to have predicted either could mean the twelfth apostle's office, which should be filled again and with which the citations from Psalms 69:25 and 109:8 in verse 20 are connected, or it could mean the betrayal and handing over of Jesus. According to the way the passage in the text is constructed, it seems that the second possibility is to be preferred.[26] If one knows that Psalm 41 played an important role in the early church's understanding of

26. Generally only the text or texts mentioned in verse 20 are considered as the Old Testament references which underlie the words "the scripture had to be fulfilled, which the Holy Spirit spoke beforehand by the mouth of David, concerning Judas." Thus, e.g., Kirsopp Lake and Henry J. Cadbury, *The Beginnings of Christianity, Part I, The Acts of the Apostles* (London: Macmillan), Vol. 4 (1933), p. 12; Alfred Wikenhauser, *Die Apostelgeschichte* (Regensburger Neues Testament [Regensburg: Verlag Friedrich Pustet, 3d ed. 1956]), pp. 33 f.

Judas, then clearly one should look for the Davidic prediction here referred to, in that Psalm with the falsehood it names. The motif encountered in Acts 1:17, that Judas was reckoned as one of Jesus' close associates, indeed fits with Psalm 41, as well as with Psalm 55:12,13. This motif also fits well with the typology which was presumably found in the early church's understanding of Judas and which will be examined more closely below.

According to the Synoptic accounts of the Last Supper, Jesus makes a prediction that one of the twelve will betray him (Mark 14:17–21 and parallel passages). In this connection it says that Jesus will go as it is written of him (Mark 14:21): "The Son of man goes as it is written of him, but woe to that man by whom the Son of man is betrayed!" The reference to scriptural prediction can be understood as applying only to Jesus' suffering and death, yet the betrayal by Judas can also be included.[27] Matthew 27:9 and Acts 1:20 show how the events involving Judas were illuminated by scriptural references. That in the passage noted above, the betrayal by Judas was also included under the aspect of scriptural fulfillment, can be seen in the significant words in Jesus' prediction, as recorded in Mark 14:18: "Truly, I say to you, one of you will betray me, *one who is eating with me.*" The last phrase is certainly cited from Psalm 41:9 (Hebrew, v. 10). Mark is the only one of the Synoptic gospels who introduces this citation. In view of its well-attested textual transmission it would seem difficult to me to disregard this phrase in Mark simply as a gloss.[28] Rather, one gets from the text of Mark an example of the fact that Psalm 41 occupied

27. See Ch. Maurer, "Knecht Gottes und Sohn Gottes im Passionsbericht des Markusevangeliums," *Zeitschrift für Theologie und Kirche* 50 (1953): 12.
28. Vincent Taylor *The Gospel According to St. Mark* (London: Macmillan, 1952), p. 540, "The fact that the phrase is wanting in Mt and the v. ll. [variant readings] in Mk suggests that it may be a gloss. . . . It is not certain, however, that the phrase is a quotation . . . , and Matthew may not have thought of it as such; it does not point to Judas as the traitor, but voices horror at the idea of treachery associated with table-fellowship." However, all of the more important manuscripts have these words from Psalm 41. In view of the great role which this Psalm played in the traditions, it seems natural to me that it was the intention of Mark to cite it.

an important place in the early church when it went about portraying Judas as the betrayer predicted in the Scripture. As a result, this scriptural interpretation was linked especially with the traditions about the Last Supper.

From what has been said it develops that there was a prevailing tendency in the early church to interpret Judas on the basis of scriptural predictions.[29] The incomprehensible events connected with the person of Judas could be understood only as important parts of God's history of salvation. The Old Testament texts which, even in details, contained predictions on Jesus' suffering and death, proved to be of such a nature that they also transmitted statements about Judas. If one can, without difficulty, understand the interpretation of Judas in the primitive church as proceeding from the Scripture, the question of Jesus' attitude toward Judas, however, still remains unsettled.

IN JESUS' OWN VIEW

It seems to me to be highly questionable to set aside all of the statements in the gospels by Jesus on Judas as unhistorical and as created after the event to illuminate the role of Judas in the narratives about Jesus.[30] The traditions are so unanimous on this point that one must reckon with their chief assertions. Among other things, this means that Jesus, at the end of his ministry, did understand the attitude of Judas—an attitude which could become ominous (Mark 14:18 and parallels). But this immediately raises the question as to why Jesus still kept this disciple near himself. Since it is probable that Jesus had some knowledge of the negotiations of Judas with the Jewish leaders, Jesus must have exhibited some reason on his part why he did not withdraw from Judas. The apostles apparently did not see in Judas a suspicious person; therefore, Jesus' hints on the betrayal were misunderstood (Matt. 26:21 ff.; Luke 22:23;

---

29. On the theme of scriptural fulfillment and Judas, see also Haugg (cited above, n. 2), p. 105; Halas (cited above, n. 7), pp. 171 ff.; Lüthi, "Das Problem des Judas Iskariot" (cited above, n. 8), pp. 102 f.

30. See G. Schläger, "Die Ungeschichtlichkeit des Verräters Judas," *Zeitschrift für die neutestamentliche Wissenschaft* 15 (1914): 50 ff.; Lüthi, *Judas Iskarioth* (cited above, n. 1), pp. 159, 166 f.

John 13:22 ff.). One should probably fit Jesus' attitude toward Judas into his view about the passion, which he went consciously to meet.[31] The gospels indicate that this understanding is correct by reference to Jesus' total view of his impending suffering as "predestined."[32] Jesus could have seen in Judas the instrument which was designated to set in motion the passion history. The important function which Judas fills in the prelude to this could be seen under the aspect of "the event foreordained by God." Several passages testify to this: Matthew 26:15,50,56; 27:9; Mark 14:49; John 17:12; 18:4.

It seems best to me to view Jesus' much discussed remark to Judas at the arrest (Matt. 26:50), *hetaire eph' ho parei,* in this connection and to translate: "My friend, (do that) for which you have come" (as it is rendered in the R.S.V. footnote).[33] Jesus sees the betrayal by Judas as a fulfillment of Scripture, a point which is underscored by Matthew 26:56, "All this has taken place, that the scriptures of the prophets might be fulfilled." John does not understand the matter differently when, in connection with the prediction of the betrayal, he has Jesus say at 13:18, "I know whom I have chosen." Therefore Jesus can have viewed Judas in light of the predestined salvation event.

31. See, for example, the three announcements of his impending suffering at Mark 8:31; 9:30 ff.; 10:32 ff.
32. Joachim Jeremias, *"pais theou,"* in G. Kittel's *Theological Dictionary of the New Testament,* ed. by Gerhard Friedrich, tr. by G. W. Bromiley (Grand Rapids: Eerdmans), Vol. 5 (1967), pp. 709–17; also, tr. by Harold Knight *et al., The Servant of God* (Studies in Biblical Theology, 20 [London: SCM, and Naperville: Allenson, 1957]), pp. 94–104; rev. ed. (1965), pp. 94–106.
33. Ernst Lohmeyer, *Das Evangelium des Matthäus,* ed. by Werner Schmauch (Meyer Kritisch-exegetischer Kommentar [Göttingen: Vandenhoeck & Ruprecht, 1958]), p. 364. "It was over that 'for which [Judas] has come' that Jesus had grappled in the midnight hour and received certainty: it is the will of God, the hour has come, the betrayer has come. These words set the seal beneath that revelation of God; he himself sets the seal; he knows, and wills, and himself assists in, that 'for which Judas has come.' Therefore, he calls him his friend. In such a context it follows also that Matthew has not added this little sentence but it belongs originally to this narrative, which is pulled together in a deep and necessary unity with what had gone before. The connection made by a relative (pronoun) ["for which," *eph'ho*] is an external sign of this greater connectedness." See also John 13:27—"Then after the morsel, Satan entered into him [Judas]. Jesus said to him, 'What you are going to do, do quickly.'"

It seems to me that it is this motif of "scriptural fulfillment" which dominates the New Testament understanding of Judas, and not the motif of greed. It follows from the New Testament texts that the motif of greed had no such great significance in the original setting as it received in later exposition.

3

THE MOTIF OF "GREED FOR MONEY"

STUDY of the gospel passages which established the idea that greed and avarice were the chief reason for the betrayal by Judas produces a surprising result: these very passages give no substantial support for such an idea. Further, as demonstrated above, the gospels do not stress among the chief features in their picture of Judas the motif that, as a lover of money, Judas sold his master for a ridiculously low price of thirty silver shekels. The passages which present Judas as greedy are only John 12:4–6 and Matthew 26:15. If one compares these, meanwhile, with their parallels in the other gospels, one can make the following observations which demonstrate that the motif of greed for money was not prominent in the original shape of the pericopes.

THE ANOINTING AT BETHANY AND JUDAS'S ACTIONS

John 12:4–6 belongs to the pericope about Jesus at Bethany: Jesus is anointed by Mary with costly nard which had a value of three hundred denarii. Judas sees this as an unthinkable waste. He protests that the ointment should rather be sold and its proceeds given to the poor. After these remarks by Judas, the evangelist injects the statement that Judas actually did not care for the poor, but wanted to put the money into his own pocket (12:6). In both of the direct parallels which Matthew 26:6–13 and Mark 14:3–9 provide for this pericope, the situation is different. There it is an unnamed woman who pours out an expensive ointment over Jesus' head. There, too, this deed provokes a protest. Judas, however, is not mentioned. According to Matthew, it is "the disciples" who protest and speak up in behalf of the poor. According to Mark, "several" (R.S.V., "there were some who said to themselves indignantly") protest. On the question as to whether at this point the Johannine or the Markan–Matthean tradition mirrors the original, one can scarcely be in doubt. John seems to me to be secondary to the "unreflected" development in Mark–Matthew. John presents Judas as the only one who protests, and on this occasion, as a parenthesis, John inserts that observation cited above. Since the Synoptic tradition does not mention Judas in this connection, the Bethany pericope does not seem to me to support the motif of greed for money.[34]

The other text, Matthew 26:14–16, portrays how Judas goes to the chief priests and offers to hand Jesus over to them. Matthew's rendition of the account underscores the greed of Judas by having him say, "What do you want to give me, if I shall betray him to you?" Thereupon follows a citation from Zechariah 11:12, which clearly has the purpose of relating the Judas-money to certain Old Testament texts. The continuation of the story is found in Matthew 27:3–10.[35] From the manner in which Matthew has Judas make his entry, one gets the impression that Judas has formally completed a business transaction. He *requests* money, in order to carry out his deed. Here, however, Mark presents a totally different form of the text: "And Judas Iscariot, one of the twelve, went to the chief priests in order to betray him to them. When they heard it they were glad, and promised to give him money" (Mark 14:10 f.). Here it sounds as if money and payment first enter into the transaction as an expression of the pleasure and thankfulness which the enemies felt in face of the amazing proposal with which Judas

34. Luke has not placed his anointing pericope at Bethany. Rather he offers a different tradition at 7:36–50. Here it is declared that a woman in the house of Simon the Pharisee anointed the feet of Jesus. This anointing has nothing to do with Jesus' burial, and the pericope does not speak of a protest by the disciples. Therefore it offers very little of interest for this discussion.

35. Matthew omits the statement which both Mark and John have, that the ointment was worth three hundred denarii. He does this apparently to give emphasis to the number thirty, the number of pieces of betrayal money.

came. There is no mention of the point that Judas was driven to his act by love of money. The Lukan version (22:3–6) does not present Judas as greedy either. There the crucial point under consideration is *how* the surrender should take place: "And he went away and conferred with the chief priests and captains *how* he might betray him to them. They were glad and offered to give him money" (Luke 22:4 f.). Luke here joins this incident with what he had said earlier, that the chief priests did not know *how* they could put Jesus to death (22:2).

Thus it becomes clear that, in the pericope on the betrayal by Judas, Matthew stresses a certain aspect of Judas, in order to be able to make a connection better with Old Testament texts in which money plays an important part, namely the thirty silver shekels.[36] Both texts which clearly present Judas as a greedy man, driven to the betrayal by his love for money, thereby show definite and intentional tendencies, in a certain connection, to illuminate *one* side of the personality of Judas, a side of which we otherwise know nothing.

If one views the motif of greed for money as only a less important tradition in the complex of Judas materials, then one asks how it was that precisely *this* side could occupy such significance in the interpretation of Judas. It is possible that it was an attempt to give a simple and rational answer to a naïve question: how was it possible that one of the twelve disciples acted so incomprehensively and betrayed Jesus? By emphasizing that he was a thief, one solved the puzzle in a satisfying way. For a reader of the gospel it was not so easy to grasp and understand the theologically more complicated conception of the place of Judas in salvation history. Moreover, in Jewish texts one finds a noteworthy connection between love of money and Satanic might.[37] This could very easily have penetrated into the New Testament texts.

36. On this tendency of Matthew, see Lüthi, "Das Problem des Judas Iskariot" (cited above, n. 8), pp. 104 f.

37. See, for example, in the Dead Sea Scrolls, Cairo Damascus Document (CD) 4.15 ff.; in the *Testaments of the XII Patriarchs,* Test. Jud. 17:1; 18:2; 19:1,2.

THE INTENT OF JUDAS (MARK 14, MATTHEW 26)

We will probably never know what really caused Judas to go to the leaders of his people with the offer to hand Jesus over. The texts tell us how Jesus and the early church might have thought about the reasons for the betrayal—Judas was part of the divine plan of salvation, already announced in the Old Testament—however, the texts tell us nothing about Judas's own motives. One can come up with nothing but speculations. After we are convinced to set aside greed as a chief motive, not much is left except to see Judas's behavior as a reaction to his disillusionment and loss of messianic hopes, a mode of behavior he had probably not expected to turn out with such consequences as it did, namely, that Jesus was put to death.[38]

Leading to this interpretation is the structure of the text at the beginning of Mark 14 and Matthew 26. First there is a brief statement about the plans nurtured by Jesus' enemies in connection with the Passover. They wanted to put Jesus to death, but did not risk it from fear of the populace. For to kill Jesus during the festival could easily lead to a riot (Mark 14:1 f.; Matt. 26:1–5). Then the anointing pericope follows (Mark 14:3–9; Matt. 26:6–13). After this there is a brief portrayal of Judas's going to the chief priests to let them know his intentions on betrayal (Mark 14:10 f.; Matt. 26:14–16). It is easy to see here how the anointing pericope was later inserted into a connected text which embraced the plans of the chief priests and the betrayal by Judas.[39] Since there is no mention of Judas in the

38. Matthew is the only one who reports that Judas felt remorse when he saw the result of his betrayal. Judas says: "I have sinned, in that I have *betrayed innocent blood (paradous haima athōon)*," 27:4. The words "innocent blood" easily turn one's thoughts to such juridical statements as Deuteronomy 27:25, "Cursed be he who takes a bribe *to slay innocent blood (pataksai psychēn haimatos athōon)*." Matthew could thereby indicate that Judas had not counted on the death of Jesus. Perhaps his purpose was only to hinder Jesus' misleading the people. The same idea could lie behind the words in Mark 14:44, "The one I shall kiss is the man; seize him and lead him away *securely (asphalōs)*." The intention was not to deliver Jesus to death, but only to put him into secure custody.

39. See, for example, Georg Bertram, *Die Leidensgeschichte Jesu und der Christuskult: eine formgeschichtliche Untersuchung* (Forschungen zur Religion und Literatur des Alten und Neuen Testaments, N. F. 15 [Göttingen: Vandenhoeck & Ruprecht, 1922]), pp. 16 ff.

Bethany pericope, the occasion for its insertion at this point is less evident. One would therefore rather place it before the entry into Jerusalem, as John does. Still, there is a possibility of finding a definite purpose expressed in Mark–Matthew for the insertion of the story of the anointing between the plans of the chief priests and the betrayal by Judas. The purpose would be a double one: to explain how Judas was able to change the plans of the chief priests not to arrest Jesus during the Passover festival; and to show how it came about that Judas went to the chief priests, whose hostile attitude toward Jesus he must have known.[40]

How can one find a motive for Judas's way of acting from the pericope about the anointing of Jesus in Bethany? First it must be remembered what purpose the anointing of Jesus had. As has been clearly shown, this pericope describes, in the form which it has in Mark, an anointing beforehand of the body of Jesus for his burial.[41] This presents a valid, legitimate substitute for the anointing of the body which could not have taken place after the execution of a condemned man. According to Mark 15:45 f., Jesus' corpse was not prepared for burial before the entombment. However, that was not a disgrace, since the anointing had already taken place: "She has anointed my body for burial beforehand," Mark 14:8. The woman in this anointing acted in a particular manner, a manner which is, according

40. See John 11:57, where one reads, "The chief priests and the Pharisees had given orders that if anyone knew where he [Jesus] was, he should let them know, so that they might arrest him."

41. J. Jeremias, "Die Salbungsgeschichte. Mark 14:3–9," *Zeitschrift für die neutestamentliche Wissenschaft* 35 (1936): 75–82, reprinted in his *Abba: Studien zur neutestamentlichen Theologie und Zeitgeschichte* (Göttingen: Vandenhoeck & Ruprecht, 1966), pp. 107–15. David Daube, *The New Testament and Rabbinic Judaism* (London: University of London, Athlone Press, 1956), p. 313: "The fundamental difference between Mark and John is that in Mark the woman anticipates, i.e. here and now performs, the burial rite of anointing, whereas in John she does not. In Mark, Jesus says of her that 'she is come aforehand to anoint my body to the burial.' The import of this ought not to be watered down: her act is boldly declared a valid, though proleptic, anointing of the body for burial. . . . On the basis of the interpretation in Mark, the burial rite of anointing has now taken place. The sources show that the Rabbis were quite familiar with acts of this sort—acts with immediate legal or religious effect, though, in reality, an essential element is still to come."

to acknowledged Jewish practice, a direct expression for an "anointing for burial."[42] She thereby carried out a work of love which was more important than alms for the poor, of which the protesting disciples were thinking. The event in Bethany was called an "anointing for burial" by Jesus himself. Accordingly, it is a part of the advance proclamations of his death which could not have escaped the attention of the disciples. The activity of the woman could have had only *one* meaning in their eyes, namely the one which Jesus expressed in his explanation: it was a "burial rite." If now Jesus showed so clearly that he would soon meet death, the disciples must have had something else to think about in place of their "crass" messianic understanding to which they had clung so long. The gospels tell that they could not understand the messianic categories in which Jesus thought. The Messiah was to raise up the poor, the pious, so they supposed, yes, "redeem Israel" (Luke 24:21).[43] How could that fit with this legally correct anointing for burial? One could very well imagine that Judas's messianic hopes finally died at this moment and that he could see no other way out than to deliver Jesus over to the chief priests. For the sake of the people, who also hoped in Jesus (Mark 14:2), Jesus had to be unmasked,[44] for now he had broken definitely with all "normal" messianic expectations.

This would be a plausible motive for Judas and his actions, a motive which was kept in the structure of the text provided by Mark and Matthew: vague plans of Jesus' enemies; an anointing at Bethany; Judas's betrayal before the chief priests—a motive which provides at the same time an acceptable explanation for precisely this arrangement of the text.

---

42. Daube (cited above, n. 41), p. 315.

43. See Paul Volz, *Die Eschatologie der jüdischen Gemeinde im neutestamentlichen Zeitalter nach der Quellen der rabbinischen, apokalyptischen und apokryphen Literatur* (Tübingen: J.C.B. Mohr, 1934), pp. 78 f., 351.

44. A. Schlatter, *Der Evangelist Matthäus* (cited above, n. 13), p. 737, writes on Matt. 26:4: "He did not go to the Romans. Judas felt as a Jew. The decision for or against Jesus is a concern within Judaism. The Christ has come to Israel. Whether he should be accepted or rejected is a matter for the Jewish community."

4

THE "DEMONOLOGY" MOTIF

THE New Testament writers were not primarily concerned with accounting for the motive which might eventually have been decisive for the actions of Judas. Rather they were concerned with fitting Judas and his deed into a theological point of view. What really lay behind his action? We have seen above that it was thus important to fit Judas into the events of salvation history and to provide the motivation under the aspect ". . . that the scripture might be fulfilled." This can be illuminated from still another side.

"SATAN ENTERED IN . . ." (LUKE 22, JOHN 13)

Luke and John do not have the same compositional construction as Mark 14 and Matthew 26 (see above, pp. 19 ff.). (Luke does not have the pericope about the anointing at Bethany, and John exhibits a different pattern than Mark–Matthew.) Luke and John must therefore know a different motivation for Judas's initiative as betrayer than the one provided by the anointing pericope. This other motivation for the betrayal has a definite theological background which is related to the motif of scriptural fulfillment. Accordingly, Luke arranges things so that, after he has spoken of the wish of the chief priests to get Jesus out of the way (22:1–2), he simply states: "Then Satan entered into Judas called Iscariot who was of the number of the twelve; he went away and conferred with the chief priests and captains how he might betray him to them" (22:3–4). It is the same in John, where it is written: "And during supper, when the devil had already put it into the heart of Judas Iscariot, Simon's son, to betray him . . ." (13:2), and "after the morsel Satan entered into him" (13:27). To judge according to these texts, Judas must be considered an important figure in the mighty conflict between the power of Satan and the power of God which took place around the person of Jesus during his passion and death. In the Lukan passion history this conflict-motif is expressed more clearly than in the other Synoptics (22:31,53). Thus, this trait is shared by Luke and John,[45] that means, in the gospels which, in place of the anointing pericope, cite Judas's possession by Satan as motive for his betrayal.

JUDAS, A SYMBOLIC FIGURE?

If one now tries to be more precise as to the role which Judas plays in this connection, one encounters a complex of problems which is far too extensive to be discussed here, but which must still be mentioned because of the importance which it has for understanding Judas in relation to the power of Satan. To be specific, Judas has on occasion been seen as a mythical figure which represents the Jewish people.[46] Even if one does not accept this mythical explanation of the figure of Judas, there still remains a certain parallelism between Judas and the Jews, a relation which especially arises from the presentation by John. There it is pointedly stressed how the Jewish people betrayed their own son Jesus, of David's lineage. When they refuse to accept him who was sent by God, this is the equivalent of betrayal (John 1:11; 5:37 f., 43; 7:27 ff.; 8:38 ff.). Pilate also stresses in Jesus' presence that it is the Jews who have delivered him into Pilate's hands: "Your people and the chief priests have handed you over to me" (18:35); 18:28.[47] One should note here the term *paradidonai,* which means "to hand over" and "to

45. See B. Noack, *Satanas and Soteria: Studien zur neutestamentlichen Soteriologie* (Copenhagen: G. E. Gad, 1948), pp. 90 f.; Lyder Brun, *Lukas Evangeliet* (Oslo: Ascheboug, 1933), pp. 516, 543.

46. See, for example, B. Schläger (cited above, n. 30), pp. 57 ff.; or Haugg, (cited above, n. 2), p. 159.

47. See Heinrich Schlier, "Jesus und Pilatus," in *Die Zeit der Kirche: exegetische Aufsätze und Vorträge* (Freiburg: Herder, 1956), pp. 61, 71.

betray," and is very significant in this connection.[48] Jesus' own people handed him over, betrayed him.

In Luke–Acts

This notion of betrayal of Jesus by the Jews, of which the betrayal by Judas forms only a part, appears again in the Lukan writings, where one reads in several texts, as a direct charge against the Jews, that they handed Jesus over. Thus, for example in Acts 3:12 ff. The scene is Solomon's portico, where Peter and John are with the lame man who was healed by Peter and with a large crowd of Jews. There Peter addresses the Jews and says: "God . . . glorified his servant (*pais*) Jesus, whom you delivered up (or betrayed, *paredōkate*) and denied in the presence of Pilate, when (although) he had decided to release him. But you denied the Holy and Righteous One and asked for a murderer to be granted to you, and you killed the Prince of life" (3:13–15a). In this text the Jews are represented as responsible for Jesus' being delivered up. This same concept also appears in Stephen's defense before the Jewish Sanhedrin or council. In it the Jews are accused as those who have betrayed Jesus: "Which of the prophets did not your fathers persecute? And they killed those who announced beforehand the coming of the Righteous One, of whom you have now become betrayers (*prodotai*) and murderers . . ." (7:52).[49] Moreover, this is a persistent theme in the preaching of the apostles in the first half of Acts: the Jews are accused of the murder of Jesus (2:23; 4:10; 5:30; 13:27 f.; cf. Luke 24:20). Certainly these references are based on old traditions, which Luke reproduces. That is evidence for the fact that the Johannine view of a certain parallelism between Judas and the Jewish people is not merely

48. Schläger (cited above, n. 30), pp. 55 f.; Karl Hermann Schelkle, *Die Passion Jesu in der Verkündigung des Neuen Testaments: ein Beitrag zur Formgeschichte und zur Theologie des Neuen Testaments* (Heidelberg: Kerle, 1949), pp. 70 ff.

49. The term *prodotēs* appears only three times in the New Testament: in Acts 7:52; in the catalogue of vices at 2 Tim. 3:4 (R.S.V., "treacherous"); and in Luke 6:16, as a designation for Judas, *Ioudas Iskariōth, hos egeneto prodotēs,* "Judas Iscariot, who became a traitor." This last passage also speaks in favor of a certain parallelism between Judas and the Jews.

the conclusion of theological speculations of a later period, but can be traced back to the proclamation of the primitive church. The important expression *paradidonai* receives its meaning from Isaiah 53, a point which emerges most clearly from the proclamation of the apostles as seen in Acts, where hints of the *pais* [servant] theology can be heard.[50] One of the motives in the *'Ebed* [Hebrew: servant]-hymns is the handing over of the righteous one to death.[51] According to primitive Christian understanding, Judas and the Jews were the instruments by which were fulfilled those plans of God indicated in the *'Ebed*-hymns (Isa. 53:6 LXX).

In the Fourth Gospel

That parallelism between Judas and the Jews is provided in John by the fact that it is said of both of them that they were inspired by Satan in their hostility to Jesus. Accordingly, Jesus says that Judas was a *diabolos*: "Did I not choose you, the twelve, and one of you is a devil?" (6:70). Yet this same charge is leveled also at the Jews when Jesus says, "You are of your father, the devil, and want to do the desires of your father. He was a murderer from the beginning and has not stood (does not stand) in the truth, for truth is not in him" (8:44).[52] It is the devil, who wants to corrupt men, who is inspiring Judas and the Jews for the attack against the one whom God sent, the Messiah. Moreover, these are the only situations in the Johannine Gospel in which the term *diabolos* appears.[53]

As shown above, we find in Luke and John a concept of Judas which traces the betrayal to inspiration by Satan. The power hostile to God uses Judas as well as the leaders of the Jews in its battle against the lordship of God. This conflict-motif is very prominent in the Gospel of John. The battle between God and

50. B. Gärtner, *"ṭly'* als Messiasbezeichnung," *Svensk Exegetisk Årsbok,* 18–19 (1953–54): 105.

51. The Septuagint uses the verb *paradidonai* in this connection: *anth' hōn paredothē eis thanaton hē psuchē autou . . . kai dia tas hamartias autōn paredothē,* Isa. 53:12. Cf. Maurer (cited above, n. 27), pp. 9, 16.

52. See Noack (cited above, n. 45), pp. 87 ff.

53. *Ibid.,* pp. 56 f.

Satan, light and darkness, here takes on powerful, cosmic proportions, when the power of Satan, which until then had held the world captive in darkness, sees its rule threatened by God's Son. This is expressed when, in connection with the betrayal, after Satan had entered into Judas, it is reported: "So, after receiving the morsel, Judas immediately went out; and it was night" (13:30). The term "night" here declares that Satan's time has come to attack the Son of God. Satan's game was especially pursued at night, according to Jewish conceptions. "The night up to the cock's crowing is generally the time of the demons."[54] In John and especially in the Qumran texts, darkness symbolizes the realm of the powers hostile to God.[55] One also finds in the passion history in Luke the view that Satan's might fights against the God's Messiah. There Jesus says to the soldiers in Gethsemane (22:53): "When I was with you day after day in the temple, you did not lay hands on me. But this is your hour and the domain of darkness." Once more the Jews appear as the instrument of the power of evil. In Jesus' passion and death, therefore, Satan plays his game, but Jesus conquers him: ". . . for the ruler of this world is coming; he has no power over me" (John 14:30b; cf. 16:11; 12:31).

That Judas, when viewed as Satan-inspired, gains tremendously in perspective, is shown also by the expression "son of perdition" at John 17:12. Here Jesus says in his high priestly prayer, "While I was with them, I kept them in your name which you have given me. I have guarded them, and none of them is lost, except the son of perdition (*ho huios tēs apōleias*), that the scripture might be fulfilled." This term "son of perdition," which occurs only *once* more in the New Testament, is in all probability taken from a specifically demonological setting. In this way the Satan-motif in the New Testament understanding of Judas is still further underscored. One will come to understand this demonological setting best from the vantage point

54. Ferdinand Weber, *Jüdische Theologie auf Grund des Talmud und verwandter Schriften* (Leipzig: Dorrfling, 1897), p. 255.
55. See, for example, Friedrich Nötscher, *Zur theologischen Terminologie der Qumran-Texte* (Bonner Biblische Beiträge, 10 [Bonn: Peter Hanstein Verlag, 1956]), pp. 92 ff., 123 ff.

of the other passage which contains the expression "son of perdition." At 2 Thessalonians 2:3, Paul describes the event which must precede the *parousia* [final coming] of Christ: "(The day of the Lord) will not come, unless the apostasy (*hē apostasia*) comes first, and the man of lawlessness (*ho anthrōpos tēs anomias*) reveals himself, the son of perdition (*ho huios tēs apōleias*). . . ." This figure, none other than the Antichrist, will raise himself up against everything that is holy, and pretend that he is God. This "man of lawlessness" or "son of perdition" is not identical with Satan, [56] but—and that is important to note— is a man (*anthrōpos*), a figure inspired and dominated by Satan, who will perform Satan's will, to entice Christians into apostasy and destruction.

The Background in Jewish Literature

In this connection it is advisable to take a side-glance at Jewish and late-Jewish literature for comparison. It is frankly very difficult to discover to which of the demonological ideas found there the New Testament attaches. According to some texts Satan is in the service of God, while according to others he is in conflict with God. The most probable background to the texts at John 17:12 and 2 Thessalonians 2:3, in which, admittedly, "son of perdition" denotes a different thing each time, are the *Testaments of the Twelve Patriarchs* and the closely related Qumran texts.[57] There Beliar (Belial) appears. He is the lord of the evil spirits, God's adversary, whose hostility to God does not manifest itself in direct conflict with God, but rather in influencing men so that they become hostile to God.[58] He inspires and entices them to apostasy and rebellion against God and thereby at the same time attacks the true Israel. Particularly in 1QH, Belial, as he is known there,[59] appears as the evil power, who

56. Noack (cited above, n. 45), pp. 119 f.: Béda Rigaux, *Les épitres aux Thessaloniciens* (Études Bibliques [Paris: Gabalda, 1956]), p. 656.
57. Noack (cited above, n. 45), pp. 33 f. Cf. G. Molin, *Die Söhne des Lichtes* (Vienna: Herold, 1954), pp. 127 ff.
58. Noack (cited above, n. 45), p. 47. Beliar is God's enemy. "Yet his hostility against God is not expressed in direct conflict against him. Rather it expresses itself in its influence on men."
59. In 1QH the name "Satan" appears only once, in fragment 4.6.

seeks to drive men to destruction and thereby makes use of the evil spirits and "impulses" which are found in these men.

Such concepts were common in the time of Jesus. From them we can see that the New Testament texts present Judas (and the leaders of the Jews—according to John) as well as the Antichrist too (2 Thess. 2:3) as men influenced and inspired by Satan, who carry out the work of the power hostile to God. It is also easy to understand the *huios tēs apōleias* at John 17:12 in these categories as one who is inspired by Beliar, as the one who is in the service of "the evil one."

That Greek phrase could be a rendering of the Hebrew *'ish beliya'al,* or Aramaic *bar beliya'al* [man or son of Belial]. The same applies to the "man of lawlessness" in 2 Thessalonians 2:3.[60] If one studies the terms appearing in this passage, one finds that in the LXX two of them, *apostasia* and *anomia* ["lawlessness"], sometimes reproduce the Hebrew *beliya'al,* which means "evil," "malice," "ruin." However, neither in the original text nor in the LXX translation of the Old Testament does *belial* assume the personified form of a Satan figure.[61] All the more, then, it is a mark of the intertestamental literature and the Qumran texts, that Beliar or Belial appears as a Satan figure. This Jewish conceptual world could very well be responsible for the appearance of the expression in the New Testament, although literally found only in one passage, namely 2 Corinthians 6:15.

If this is so, one could venture the conjecture that in John 17:12 and 2 Thessalonians 2:3 a late Jewish Beliar-concept is reflected, which developed from the Old Testament word *beliya'al.* This fits well in the passage from Psalm 41, which was related above to Judas in connection with John 13:18. In Psalm 41:8 (Hebrew, 41:9) we read, "A deadly thing is poured out over him; he who lies down will not rise again." The man offering this liturgical prayer here reproduces what his enemy is thinking about him. According to his enemy's wish, what should

60. See Rigaux (cited above, n. 56), pp. 656 f.
61. Noack (cited above, n. 45), pp. 58 f.

strike the suffering righteous man is a "deadly thing," *d^ebar-b^eliya'al,* "a deed of Belial," a "deed of perdition."

Since the connection between the Johannine understanding of Judas and Psalm 41 is clear, the Johannine "son of perdition" therefore also fits extremely well in this situation. Judas is one who belongs to the circle of Beliar, who in his betrayal is in the service of Beliar, inspired by him.[62] In *4Q Testimonia* a satanically inspired man also appears. As such, he misleads the people and sets himself up against the "messiah" of the sect. He is called *'ish b^eliya'al.*[63] This speaks for the possibility of fitting Judas into a world of late Jewish demonological concepts and of interpreting the "son of perdition" in the way done above.

62. J. S. Billings, "Judas Iscariot in the Fourth Gospel," *Expository Times* 51 (1939–40): 156 f., conceives Judas, the son of perdition, as Satan incarnate. Billings makes a connection with C. H. Dodd's thesis of "realized eschatology" and asserts that the son of perdition in 2 Thess. 2:3 "was not to be expected in the future, but had already appeared and had been incarnate in Judas Iscariot."

63. J. M. Allegro, "Further Messianic References in Qumran Literature," *JBL* 75 (1956): 185. "Then he [Joshua] said, *'Cursed be the man who builds this city; with his firstborn shall he lay its foundation, and with his last-born shall be set up its gates'* [Josh. 6:26]. And, behold a man accursed, the devil's own (literally, "the one of Belial"; read, *u^ehinnēh 'ish 'ārûr 'ahad b^eliya'al*) shall arise, to be a fowl[er's sn]are to his people and destruction to all his neighbors" (4Q test. 22–24). There is evident a certain parallelism between this figure known to a sect and the New Testament Antichrist.

5

JUDAS TYPOLOGY IN THE NEW TESTAMENT

T HE New Testament texts show how Jesus and the primitive church viewed Judas and his deed. They do this in two ways: they describe his betrayal as predicted in Scripture, and they portray him as inspired by Satan. These two closely related motifs lead us into a primitive Christian typology about Judas which assigns him a place that has little to do with the popular concept of "Judas, the greedy one." This typology is, however, not completely clear, since it is preserved only in fragmentary form. One has the feeling that there could have been a number of concepts about Judas which were lost already at an early stage. This probably happened above all in the first years after the death and resurrection of Jesus, as the attempt was made to fit Judas and his action into the event of salvation history.

AHITHOPHEL AS A TYPE

In this typological connection I want to call attention now to a figure who has been ignored all too much in exegetical studies of Judas. In Jewish circles he played a role similar in part to that of Judas; in Jewish texts he strikingly resembles the New Testament presentation of Judas. The reference is to Ahithophel, who, according to 2 Samuel, was part of King David's innermost circle. He was a widely trusted person, David's counselor, and a man of great respect. It is said of him: "In those days the counsel Ahithophel gave was as if a man (or someone) asked the oracle (Hebrew, word) of God; and so was all Ahithophel's counsel respected, as by David, so by Absalom," 2

Samuel 16:23. However, the trusted one became a traitor: David's trusted friend went over to Absalom's side and swore allegiance to him against David, to get him out of the way. In this betrayal Ahithophel went so far as to encourage Absalom to go in to his father's concubines, in order thereby to demonstrate his complete assumption of power in David's place. Yet, as is recorded further in 2 Samuel, God finally confounded Ahithophel's plans against David. For Absalom declined to accept Ahithophel's final and most clever advice for getting rid of David, 2 Samuel 17:1 ff. Thus David was able to escape. However, Ahithophel was reduced to such despair, when he saw that his advice was not taken, that he rode home to his own city, "set his house in order," and hanged himself, 2 Samuel 17:23.

In rabbinic texts one encounters two persons who are displayed as traitors through and through: Balaam—as a traitor from the heathen; and Ahithophel[64]—as a man who, in the most scandalous manner, betrayed David and his own people, the people of God.[65] There are a number of other ideas which are connected with Ahithophel, such as his great wisdom, which approached that of the angels,[66] and his astrological knowledge, which he used in his attempt to manipulate the royal throne in his own interest.[67] Yet in our situation, where we are concerned

---

64. Numbers Rabba 22.7, Eng. tr. by Judah J. Slotki, in *Midrash Rabbah,* ed. by H. Freedman and Maurice Simon (London: Soncino Press, 1939 [hereafter cited as "Freedman-Simon"]), Vol. 6, *Numbers* II, p. 859. See Ginzberg, *Legends of the Jews* (cited above, n. 16), Vol. 3 (1911), pp. 354 ff. on Balaam; and on Balaam and Ahithophel, p. 414, cf. 375 and n. 771 on it in Vol. 6, p. 132.

65. Genesis Rabba 32.1, Eng. tr. by H. Freedman in Freedman-Simon (cited above, n. 64), Vol. 1, *Genesis* I, p. 249; Numbers Rabba 18.17 (Freedman-Simon, p. 729) and 19.2 (Freedman-Simon, p. 746); Ecclesiastes Rabba 10.2, Eng. tr. by A. Cohen in Freedman-Simon, Vol. 8, *Ruth-Ecclesiastes,* p. 261; Targum on Psalm 140:10. See Ginzberg, *Legends of the Jews* (cited above, n. 16), Vol. 6, p. 242.

66. See Ginzberg (cited above, n. 16), Vol. 6, pp. 256 f.

67. Babylonian Talmud tractate *Sanhedrin* 101a, Eng. tr. in *The Babylonian Talmud,* ed. by Isidore Epstein (London: Soncino Press [hereafter cited as "Epstein"]), *Seder Nezikim, Sanhedrin,* Vol. 2, tr. by H. Freedman (1935), p. 689. Babylonian Talmud tractate *Sotah* 21a. Eng. tr. by A. Cohen in Epstein, *Seder Nashim, Sotah* (1936), pp. 106 f. See M. Guttman, "Ahithophel," *Encyclopaedia Judaica* (1928–34), Vol. 1, col. 734.

about a comparison with Judas Iscariot, the betrayal motif interests us most of all.

"Betrayal"

If one studies the commentaries and descriptions which occur in the rabbinic texts about Ahithophel and his betrayal, one finds certain striking parallels with the Judas figure. Several times in these texts, in connection with Ahithophel's betrayal of David, 2 Samuel 17:2 is mentioned. According to this biblical passage, Ahithophel gave Absalom the correct advice, that Ahithophel should go out against David at once and put him to death. Absalom, however, did not follow this advice and, therefore, his revolutionary plans miscarried. The text says: "I will set out and pursue David tonight. I will come upon him while he is weary and discouraged, and throw him into a panic; and all the people who are with him will flee," 2 Samuel 17:1b,2.[68] These words of Ahithophel remind one well of the situation involving the cunning procedure of Judas that night in Gethsemane: Judas fell upon Jesus when he was weakest, and all of the disciples fled and left him alone.

"By My Trusted Friend"

Another motif which appears in the Jewish interpretation of Ahithophel stresses strongly what deceit, what trickery lay behind his deed. This is the fact that he was one of David's closest friends, one of David's inner circle. Here we have the same theme which also appears in the New Testament presentation of Judas. It is said several times of Judas that he was "one of the twelve," "he was numbered among us," Luke 22:3; Acts 1:17; Matthew 26:47; John 13:21 ff. For our consideration here the most important rabbinic text is in the Babylonian Talmud, tractate *Sanhedrin* 106b (ed. by Epstein [cited above, n. 67], p. 729), where we read: "R[abbi] Joḥanan also said: At first David called Ahithophel his teacher, then his companion [col-

---

68. Genesis Rabba 38.1. Eng. tr. in Freedman-Simon (cited above, n. 64), *Genesis* I, p. 302. Numbers Rabba 11.3, Eng. tr. in Freedman-Simon, *Numbers* I, p. 420. Song of Songs Rabba 3.7.5, Eng. tr. by M. Simon in Freedman-Simon, Vol. 9, *Song of Songs,* p. 164.

league], and finally his disciple. At first he called him his teacher, as it is written, *But it was thou, a man mine equal, my* guide [actually, friend], *and mine acquaintance* [Ps. 55:13 (Hebrew, v. 14)]. Then his companion, [as it is written] *We took sweet counsel together, and walked into the house of God in* company [Ps. 55:14 (Hebrew, v. 15)]. Finally his disciple—*Yea, mine own familiar friend, in whom I trusted,* which did eat of my bread, *hath lifted up his heel against me* [Ps. 41:9 (Hebrew, v. 10)]." What arrests our attention in this group of passages is the dominant theme that the close friend is a traitor, as well as the references to Psalm 41:9 and 55:13 f. The same reference which was considered appropriate for Judas's betrayal (Psalm 41:9), emerges here in a similar connection. John stresses the fact that Judas was present the whole time in the great communion which was expressed in the Passover meal. Yet in spite of this he was a traitor. In the rabbinic text in the tractate *Sanhedrin* the expression "he who eats my bread" represents a metaphor for "he who learned from my instruction," while John 13 and Mark 14 deal with a concrete reference to the Last Supper. However, the theme that comes from Psalm 41:9 is the same.

Psalm 41 has the same important place in the "betrayer section" of the Qumran Thanksgiving Hymns, at 1QH5. 22–28, where the "I" of the sect's hymn complains that even his companions who were in covenant with him have betrayed him, inspired as they are by Belial. "But I became . ? . [. . .] . ? . (an object of) discord and strife (? an affront) for my friends, (an object of) jealousy and anger for those who entered into my covenant, (an object of) murmuring and grumbling for all who had come to agreement with me, and [. . .] those *who* [*e*]*at my bread raise their heel against me* and slander me with malicious lips, all who were part of my circle . . . . and they plot the mischief of their heart, [. . . B]elial, they loosen the tongue of falsehood [*sheqer!*] like the poison of serpents which breaks forth. . . ." In Jewish conceptions Psalm 41 clearly played an important role in describing falsehood or betrayal (*sheqer*) against God's people.

The other psalm which is referred to in the *Sanhedrin* text is Psalm 55. This appears in various other passages with reference to Ahithophel's betrayal.[69] The similarity between Psalms 41 and 55 is very great so far as motifs go, and it seems highly probable to me that Psalm 55 also could have held a place in Judas typology. The emphasis, particularly in Luke 22:3 and Acts 1:17, that Judas belonged to Jesus' inner circle, can be a reference to that theme so prominent in Psalm 55:13 f. There are also other details which fit with this situation.

The Traitor's Suicide

This Psalm 55 appears several times with reference to another "Ahithophel motif" which should be compared with Judas. This is Ahithophel's suicide.[70] Ahithophel was counted among a group of eternally lost men which consisted of three kings and four ordinary mortals.[71] The verse at Psalm 55:23

69. See, for example, Babylonian Talmud, tractate *Aboth* 6.3, Eng. tr. by J. Israelstam in Epstein (cited above, n. 67), *Seder Nezikim* VIII, *Aboth*, pp. 80–82: "When someone learns a passage, a teaching, a line of writing, or even one letter from his fellow, he must show him honor. For so we find it with David, the king of Israel. He had learned only two things from Ahithophel, yet he calls him his master, his companion, and his familiar friend, as it is written: 'You, a man like me, my companion and my familiar friend . . .' " (Psalm 55).

Numbers Rabba 18.17, Eng. tr. in Freedman-Simon (cited above, n. 64), p. 728: " 'For it is not my enemy who reviles me, then I could bear it; it is not my hater who deals insolently with me, then I could hide from him' [Ps. 55:12 (Hebrew, v. 13)]. This alludes to Doeg and Ahithophel who reviled David. They were not, said he, my enemies, but they reviled me. They did not call me by name, but they could say, for example, 'Why does not Jesse's son come?' [1 Sam. 20:27], or 'I have seen Jesse's son' [1 Sam. 22:9], or 'Behold, I have seen a son of Jesse' [1 Sam. 16:18]. That means: 'For it is not my enemy who reviles me, then I could bear it. No, you, a man of my rank, my friend (*'alûphî*)' [Ps. 55:13 (Hebrew, v. 14)]. *'Alûphî* means that he [Ahithophel] was an outstanding scholar learned in Torah. 'And my friend (*meyuddā'î*)' [Ps. 55:13 (Hebrew, v. 14)]. He was called *meyuddā'î*) because he could pursue discussion on questions of the law."

70. Babylonian Talmud, tractate *Baba Bathra* 147a, Eng. tr. by Israel W. Slotki in Epstein (cited above, n. 67), *Seder Nezikim, Baba Bathra* II (1935), p. 635; *Sanhedrin* 69b, Eng. tr. in Epstein, p. 471; *Makkoth* 11a, Eng. tr. by H. M. Lazarus in Epstein, *Seder Nezikim, Makkoth* (1935), pp. 73 f.

71. Jeroboam, Ahab, Manasseh, Balaam, Doeg, Ahithophel, and Gehazi. See Jerusalem Talmud tractate *Sanhedrin* 10,2.

(Hebrew, v. 24) is said to refer to Ahithophel and Doeg: "But you, O God, will cast them down into the lowest pit; men of blood and treachery shall not live out half their days." A confirmation of the weight which Psalm 55 had in late Judaism, when it came to describing and commenting on the life and work of Ahithophel, is conveyed by the Targum on Psalm 55. There the central section of the Psalm is applied directly to Ahithophel. "In the midst of it [the town] oppression and fraud (*sheqar*) prevail, (55:11, Hebrew, v. 12) in the midst revolt rules, and from its streets fraud (*sheqar*) does not depart nor cunning; (55:12, Hebrew, v. 13) yet it is not my enemy who reviles me, I could bear that; it is not my hater, who raises himself against me, I could hide myself from him; (55:13, Hebrew, v. 14) no, it is you, Ahithophel, my equal, a teacher, who instructed me and imparted wisdom to me . . .; (55:15, Hebrew, v. 16) he declares them to be deserving of death and decides on evil for them, for Doeg and Ahithophel, for they should depart to the realm of the dead, while they are still living, since evil dwells in their houses, in their bodies!" One can see that the same tradition about Ahithophel which occurred in the *Sanhedrin* text appears here again. It stresses that it is the intimate friend who practices treachery. Thus in the Targum on Psalm 55 Ahithophel's name and work are read into the psalm text—so intimately were this person and his treachery linked with Psalm 55 in Jewish traditions. That strengthens the feeling that this Psalm too belonged to the Judas traditions, as did Psalm 41. At any rate, both of these Psalms belonged close together, in a specific circle of motifs which is very important for the understanding of Judas.[72]

Sorrow unto Death

Meanwhile, there is a further detail in Matthew and Mark, in the passages on Judas's betrayal, which could serve as evidence for the thesis that Psalm 55 was also claimed by the Judas typology. In the Gethsemane pericope we read, according to

72. Other texts also belong here, such as Numbers Rabba 18.17, Eng. tr. in Freedman-Simon (cited above, n. 64), *Numbers* II, pp. 728 f.; and Ecclesiastes Rabba 10.1-2, Eng. tr. in Freedman-Simon, *Ecclesiastes,* pp. 260 f.

Mark 14:33 f. (Matthew 26:37:f.): "And he took with him Peter and James and John, and began to be greatly distressed and troubled. And he said to them, 'My soul is very sorrowful, even to death (*perilupos estin hē psuchē mou heōs thanatou*).'" This saying of Jesus has generally been seen as a citation of, or a reference to, Psalm 42:5 and 11 (LXX Psalm 41:6,12),[73] where one reads: "Why are you downcast, my soul, why are you so restless in me? (*hina ti perilupos ei, psuchē, kai hina ti suntarasseis me*;)." Admittedly, though, this Psalm makes no mention of the phrase "(even) to death (*heōs thanatou*)" which is prominent in Jesus' statement. This point, however, is clearly spelled out in Psalm 55:4 f. (LXX Psalm 54:5 f.), where we read: "My heart is disturbed in me, and the terrors of death have fallen upon me (*hē kardia mou etarachthē en emoi, kai deilia thanatou epepesen ep' eme*)." It therefore seems to me not impossible to hear a hint of Psalm 55 too in Jesus' saying, for we find there the basic theme of the entire Gethsemane pericope: the fervent prayer of the Righteous One in the face of fear of death (55:2–7), as well as anxiety in the face of betrayal by a close friend (vv. 10–16); in addition, there is also the fact that this Psalm was widely used in Jewish typology about a betrayer. Let it also be noted that in the Targum to Psalm 55 three times in the decisive section the important word *sheqar*, "fraud," appears, which we also find in the surname "Iscariot."[74]

The Traitor's Fate

As reward for his betrayal, sudden death and eternal damnation were prescribed by Jewish traditions about Ahithophel.[75] In this regard Ahithophel's suicide provides a parallel to the tragic end of Judas. Both persons, after they became aware of their misfortune, went and hanged themselves, 2 Samuel 17:23 and Matthew 27:5. It is interesting to note not merely that di-

73. See, for example, V. Taylor, *The Gospel According to St. Mark* (cited above, n. 28), pp. 552 f.

74. Targum on Psalm 55:4,11,12.

75. Babylonian Talmud, tractate *Sanhedrin* 69b, 106b, Eng. tr. in Epstein (cited above, n. 67), pp. 471, 729.

rect parallel as to the manner of death, but also the fact that the New Testament has two different traditions about Judas's death. According to the second tradition (Acts 1:18), Judas "fell headlong and burst open, and all his entrails poured out." It is impossible to say whether, and in how far, the narrative in 2 Samuel 17:23 on how Ahithophel died, influenced the Judas tradition. Both New Testament accounts probably belonged to traditions about Judas which were of a more popular nature. Both were built on Old Testament motifs. Therefore, one can only say that both express the idea commonly found about the end of traitors and godless men.[76]

In the group of motifs in the Psalter about the "enemies of the righteous man" one encounters precisely the concepts which become so characteristic in the traditions built around Ahithophel and Judas. Psalms 69 and 109 are cited in Acts 1:20 as predictions for the death of Judas. Here we see the concept that the betrayer should not share in the eternal kingdom: "Let them be blotted out of the book of the living and let them not be enrolled among the righteous!" (Psalm 69:28). Here we have continuing application of what the rabbinic texts apply to Ahithophel: he shall not be resurrected, he shall not be judged, and he shall have no part in the world to come.[77] Here too the thought belongs that the betrayer should no longer be remembered in the afterlife: "May his future be cut off (or: his posterity perish), may his name be blotted out in the next generation!" Psalm 109:13.[78] So, too Wisdom of Solomon 4:18 f., where we might have the background for the description which

76. P. Benoit, "La mort de Judas," in *Synoptische Studien: Alfred Wikenhauser zum siebzigsten Geburtstag . . . dargebracht* (Munich: Karl Zink Verlag, 1953), pp. 18 f.

77. Babylonian Talmud, tractate *Ḥagigah* 15b, Eng. tr. by I. Abrahams in Epstein (cited above, n. 67), *Seder Mo'ed, Ḥagigah* (1938), p. 99. Genesis Rabba 32.1, Eng. tr. in Freedman-Simon (cited above, n. 64), *Genesis* I, p. 249. See Ginzberg, *Legends of the Jews* (cited above, n. 16), Vol. 6, pp. 242 f.

78. Genesis Rabba 38.1, Eng. tr. in Freedman-Simon (cited above, n. 64), *Genesis* I, p. 302. Numbers Rabba 22.7, Eng. tr. in Freedman-Simon, *Numbers* II, p. 859.

Acts gives for the manner of Judas's death.[79] This theme, too, appears in the statements about Ahithophel, when it is declared that the next generation should forget him. One could ask whether this theme is not echoed also in John 17:12 when it is said of the "son of perdition" that he "has been lost": ". . . I have kept them in your name which you have given me; I have guarded them, and none of them *is lost,* except the son of perdition, that the scripture might be fulfilled." If this is referred back to the Old Testament, this can well reflect the Ahithophel tradition; the betrayer is lost forever. Like Ahithophel and the other Old Testament betrayers, Balaam and Doeg, Judas is also lost. One should also note that the rather infrequently used Hebrew word (*sheqer*) appears in both Psalms which are referred to in Acts 1:20 as Judas texts—in Psalm 69:4 (Hebrew, 69:5) and 109:2. This is also the same word which underlies "Iscariot." We have now encountered it a number of times in this context. Moreover, Psalm 69 belongs to the central Old Testament material which is interwoven in the history of Jesus' passion.

The Demonic

Even the demonic trait in the figure of the betrayer, which was so striking in the case of Judas, appears in the case of Ahithophel. His knowledge was said to be not like that of a mortal, but was close to that of an angel.[80] Further in 2 Samuel 16:23 is added: "In those days the counsel Ahithophel gave was as if *someone* asked (the word of) God." It should be noted that the Hebrew consonantal text does not include *'ish,* the word rendered above by "someone." This is rather omitted. On the other hand, the Masoretes by their vocalization of the text and the corresponding marginal note inserted an *'ish*="a man," "some-

79. Wisdom of Solomon 4:19: "After this, they will become corpses, dishonored and an outrage among the dead forever. The Lord will dash them down headlong, speechless. He will shake them from their foundations, they will be utterly laid waste, anguish will be theirs, and memory of them will perish." Cf. K. Lake, "The Death of Judas," in *The Beginnings of Christianity* (cited above, n. 26), Vol. 5 (1933), pp. 29 f.

80. Ginzberg (cited above, n. 16), Vol. 6, p. 256, n. 62.

one," with the note "read 'a man,' 'someone,' but do not write it." On this, Jerusalem Talmud *Sanhedrin* 10.2 comments: "For the word 'someone,' the text does not contain the expression 'man,' since the text could not designate him as a man."

SUMMARY

It develops from the material presented above that a number of traits in the Judas tradition have parallels in the rabbinic sayings about Ahithophel. These similarities do not need to mean that there is dependence in one direction or the other. Yet they show that there are a number of traits in the Judas traditions current in the primitive church which fit well into the "betrayer categories" which the Jews took from the Old Testament Scriptures. This applied especially with reference to certain psalm texts which were of great significance for the Jewish traditions about Ahithophel.[81]

Thus, we see that the texts about Judas in the New Testament are part of a definite scriptural complex, which includes definite texts and a definite judgment on the betrayal. This helps us to penetrate the New Testament understanding of Judas better and makes it possible for us to reconstruct partially the primitive Christian typology about Judas which has largely been lost. There must have been a number of Old Testament texts which were interpreted in light of the person and deeds of Judas and of which only hints and echoes remain in the New Testament. Yet this helps us also to understand that the motif of "greed" has no great place in the portrayal of Judas. Fulfillment of Scripture and Judas as a man inspired by Satan are much more prominent themes.

81. See. for example, Deuteronomy Rabba 6.11 (Eng. tr. in Freedman-Simon [cited above, n. 64], *Deuteronomy,* tr. by J. Rabbinowitz [1951], pp. 127–29), where Moses laments over Aaron, because Aaron and Miriam grumbled against Moses. This falsehood of Aaron is also illuminated by Psalm 41:9. In Numbers Rabba 18.17, Psalm 55 is used in this connection regarding Aaron (Eng. tr. in Freedman-Simon [cited above, n. 64], pp. 728 f.).

For Further Reading

Where articles, especially those in languages other than English, have been summarized in *New Testament Abstracts,* reference is given by volume number and item number in *NT Abstracts.*

By Bertil Gärtner:

The Areopagus Speech and Natural Revelation. Tr. by Carolyn Hannay King. Acta Seminarii Neotestamentici Upsaliensis, 21. Uppsala: Almqvist & Wiksells; Lund: C.W.K. Gleerup; Copenhagen: Einar Munksgaard, 1955.

Sjukdom och lidande i Nya Testamentet. Lund: Diakonistyrelse, 1958.

John 6 and the Jewish Passover. Coniectanea Neotestamentica, 17. Uppsala: Almqvist & Wiksells; Lund: C.W.K. Gleerup; Copenhagen: Einar Munksgaard, 1959.

The Theology of the Gospel According to Thomas. Tr. by Eric J. Sharpe. New York: Harper, 1961. British edition, *The Theology of the Gospel of Thomas.* Swedish, *Ett nytt evangelium? Thomas—evangeliets hemliga Jesusord.* Stockholm: Diakonistyrelse, 1960.

The Temple and the Community in Qumran and the New Testament: A Comparative Study in the Temple Symbolism of the Qumran Texts and the New Testament. Society for New Testament Studies Monograph Series, 1. New York: Cambridge University Press, 1965.

Svensk Bibliskt Uppslags Verk, ed. by Ivan Engnell. 2 vols. Stockholm: Nordiska Uppslagsböker, 1962–63. Some forty articles, including "Judas Iskariot," Vol. 1, cols. 1251–53.

"Missionspredikan i Apostlagärningarna." *Svensk Exegetisk Årsbok* 15 (1950): 34–54.

"ṭly' als Messiasbezeichnung." *Svensk Exegetisk Årsbok* 18–19 (1953–54): 98–108.

"The Habakkuk Commentary DSH and the Gospel of Matthew." *Studia Theologica* 8 (1954): 1–24.

"Judas Iskariot." *Svensk Exegetisk Årsbok* 21 (1956): 50–81 (Swedish). *NT Abstracts* 3:51.

Die rätselhaften Termini Nazoräer und Iskariot. Horae Soederblomianae (Travaux publiés par la Société Nathan Söderblom), 4. Uppsala, 1957, distributed by C.W.K. Gleerup, Lund.

"Vilken karaktär hade Jesu sista måltid?" *Svensk Exegetisk Årsbok* 22–23 (1957–58): 87–97. *NT Abstracts* 3:557.

"Evangelium Veritatis och Nya testamentet." *Religion och Bibel* 17 (1958): 54–70.

"Bakgrunden till Qumranförsamlingens krig." *Religion och Bibel* 19 (1960): 35–72.

"L'Eucharistie et l'agneau pascal." *Välsignelsens Kalk.* Ed. by E. Segelberg. Saltsjöbaden: Kyrkligt Forum, 1961. Pp. 27–38.

"Work in the New Testament." *Svensk Exegetisk Årsbok* 26 (1961): 13–18. *NT Abstracts* 7:744.

"Qumran, Templet, Kristus." *Religion och Bibel* 21 (1962): 3–22.

"Paulus und Barnabas in Lystra. Zu Apg 14, 8–15." *Svensk Exegetisk Årsbok* 27 (1962): 83–88.

"Miljö och församling i Korint." *Festschrift for Bo Giertz.* Uppsala, 1965. Pp. 139–54.

"The Pauline and Johannine Idea of 'to know God' against the Hellenistic Background. The Greek Philosophical Principle 'Like by Like' in Paul and John." *New Testament Studies* 14 (1967–68): 209–31.

"The Person of Jesus and the Kingdom of God." *Theology Today* 27 (1970): 32–43. *NT Abstracts* 15:90.

"The Words of Institution." *Lutherans and Catholics in Dialogue, III: The Eucharist as Sacrifice.* New York: U.S.A. National Committee for the Lutheran World Federation, and Washington, D.C.: United States Catholic Conference for the Bishops' Committee for Ecumenical and Interreligious Affairs, 1967. Pp. 75–79.

"Ämbetet, mannen och kvinnan i Nya testamentet." Lund: C.W.K. Gleerup, 1958. Originally in *Kvinnan och ämbetet enligt Skriften och Bekännelse,* by Bo Reicke, *et al.* (Stockholm: Diakonistyrelse, 1958). On the ordination-of-women issue. German tr. by G. Stoll, "Das Amt, der Mann und die Frau" (Ergersheim, Bavaria: Selbstverlag Ernst Seybold, 1963), also in *In Signo Crucis* (Uppsala, 1963).

(with Gerhard Krodel) "The Lordship of Christ in the New Testament." In *Christian Hope and the Lordship of Christ.* Ed. by Martin J. Heinecken. Minneapolis: Augsburg Publishing House, 1969. Pp. 1–19.

On the Subject of This Book:

In addition to the titles below, additional older literature is listed in the *Index to Periodical Literature on Christ and the Gospels,* compiled under the direction of Bruce M. Metzger (New Testament Tools and Studies, 6 [Grand Rapids: Eerdmans, 1962]), items 525–32 and 1406–1408; in *A Classified Bibliography of Literature on the Acts of the Apostles,* compiled by A. J. Mattill, Jr., and Mary Bedford Mattill (New Testament Tools and Studies, 7 [Grand Rapids: Eerdmans, 1966]), items 4736–55; in the article on "Judas Iscariote" by H. Leclercq in the *Dictionnaire d'Archéologie Chrétienne et de Liturgie,* ed.

by F. Cabrol and H. Leclercq (Paris: Letouzey), Vol. 8 (1928), cols. 255–79, especially note 3; as well as in, of course, standard commentaries on Acts and the Synoptics.

General Surveys on Judas

BLAIR, E. P. "Judas Iscariot." *The Interpreter's Dictionary of the Bible.* New York and Nashville: Abingdon, 1962. Vol. 2, pp. 1006–1008.

FASCHER, ERICH. "Judas Iskarioth." *Die Religion in Geschichte und Gegenwart.* 3d ed. Tübingen: J.C.B. Mohr. Vol. 3 (1959), cols. 965–66.

HALAS, ROMAN B. *Judas Iscariot. A Scriptural and Theological Study of his Person, his Deeds and his Eternal Lot.* Catholic University of America, Studies in Sacred Theology, 96. Washington, D.C.: Catholic University of America Press, 1946.

HAUGG, DONATUS. *Judas Iskarioth in den neutestamentlichen Berichten.* Freiburg im Breisgau: Herder, 1930. Dissertation, University of Munich. Bibliography, pp. 11–18.

TASKER, J. G. "Judas Iscariot." *A Dictionary of Christ and the Gospels.* Ed. by James Hastings. Edinburgh: T. & T. Clark, and New York: Scribner's, 1911. Vol. 1, pp. 907–13.

VAN UNNIK, W. C. "Iskarioth." *Biblisch-Historisches Handwörterbuch.* Göttingen: Vandenhoeck & Ruprecht. Vol. 2 (1964), col. 781.

Judas in the History of Interpretation

(Titles chronologically arranged)

WREDE, WILLIAM. "Judas Iscarioth in der christlichen Überlieferung." *Vorträge und Studien.* Tübingen: J.C.B. Mohr, 1907. Pp. 127–46.

BAUER, WALTER. *Das Leben Jesu im Zeitalter der neutestamentlichen Apokryphen.* Tübingen: J.C.B. Mohr, 1909; reprinted, Darmstadt: Wissenschaftlichen Buchgesellschaft, 1967. Pp. 173–76.

HENNECKE, E. *New Testament Apocrypha.* Ed. by W. Schneemelcher. Tr. ed. by R. McL. Wilson. Philadelphia: Westminster. Vol. 1 (1963), pp. 313 f. (Gospel of Judas), pp. 505–507 (Gospel of Bartholomew). Vol. 2 (1965), pp. 62–64 (general references); cf. index.

LAEUCHLI, SAMUEL. "Origen's Interpretation of Judas Iscariot." *Church History* 22 (1953): 253–68.

CREIZENBACH, TH. *Judas Iscarioth in Legende und Sage des Mittelalters.* Halle, 1875.

BAUM, PAULL FRANKLIN. "The Mediaeval Legend of Judas Iscariot." *Publications of the Modern Language Association of America,* N.S. 31 (1916): 481–632. Bibliography.

Rand, Edward K. "Mediaeval Lives of Judas Iscariot." *Anniversary Papers, by Colleagues and Pupils of George Lyman Kittredge. . . .* Boston: Ginn & Co., 1913. Pp. 305–16.

Lüthi, Kurt. *Judas Iskariot in der Geschichte der Auslegung von der Reformation bis in die Gegenwart.* Zürich: Zwingli Verlag, 1955.

Enslin, Morton S. "How the Story Grew—Judas in Fact and Fiction." *Festschrift for F. W. Gingrich.* Ed. by Eugene H. Barth (in press).

Porte, Wilhelm. *Judas Ischarioth in der bildenden Kunst.* Berlin, 1883.

"Lives" of Judas, Sermons

Carey, S. Pearce. *Jesus and Judas.* London: Hodder & Stoughton, 1931.

Dillon, Philip Robert. *Judas of Kerioth, A Romance of Old Judea.* New York: Exposition Press, 1953.

Lévitt, Albert. *Judas Iscariot: An Imaginative Autobiography.* Hancock, New Hampshire: Flagstone Publications, 1961.

Nicole, Albert. *Judas the Betrayer.* Grand Rapids: Baker Book House, 1957.

Page, G. A. *The Diary of Judas Iscariot or the Gospel according to Judas.* London, 1912.

Van Heurn, Anton and Elly. *Judas.* Philadelphia: Muhlenberg Press, 1958.

Weatherhead, Leslie D. "Judas," in *Personalities in the Passion: A Devotional Study of Some of the Characters Who Played a Part in the Drama of Christ's Passion and Resurrection.* New York and Nashville: Abingdon-Cokesbury, 1943. Pp. 26–39.

Specialized Studies on Judas

Bacon, Benjamin W. "What Did Judas Betray?" *Hibbert Journal* 19 (1920–21) : 476–93.

Benoit, Pierre, O.P. "La morte de Judas." *Synoptischen Studien: Alfred Wikenhauser zum siebzigsten Geburtstag am 22. Februar 1953 dargebracht von Freunden, Kollegen und Schülern.* Munich: Karl Zink Verlag, 1953. Pp. 1–19.

Bishop, E. F. F. " 'Guide to Those who Arrested Jesus.' " *Evangelical Quarterly* 40 (1968) : 41 f. *NT Abstracts* 12:936.

Celada, B. "El nombre de 'Iscariote.' " *Cultura Biblica* (Segovia) 23 (1967) : 41. *NT Abstracts* 12:88.

Cox, W. A. "Judas Iscariot." *Interpreter* 3 (1907) : 414–22; 4 (1908) : 218 f.

Cullmann, Oscar. "Le douzième apôtre." *Revue d'histoire et de philosophie religieuses* (Strasbourg), 42 (No. 2–3, Mélanges Henri Clavier, 1962) : 133–40. German, "Der Zwölfte Apostel," in *Oscar Cullmann: Vorträge und Aufsätze 1925–1962,* ed. by Karlfried

Fröhlich (Tübingen: J.C.B. Mohr, and Zürich: Zwingli Verlag, © 1966), pp. 214–22.

GROSSOUW, W. K. "A Note on John xiii 1–3." *Novum Testamentum* 8 (1966): 124–31. *NT Abstracts* 11:766.

HARRIS, RENDEL. "Did Judas Really Commit Suicide?" *American Journal of Theology* 4 (1900): 490–513.

——. "St. Luke's Version of the Death of Judas." *American Journal of Theology* 18 (1914): 127–31.

HARRISON, EVERETT F. "Jesus and Judas." *Bibliotheca Sacra* 105 (1948): 170–81.

HEIN, KENNETH. "Judas Iscariot: Key to the Last Supper Narratives?" *New Testament Studies* 17 (1970–71): 227–32.

HERBER, J. "La mort de Judas." *Revue de l'Histoire des Religions* 129 (1945): 47–56.

INGHOLT, HARALD. "The Surname of Judas Iscariot." *Studia orientalia Ioanni Pedersen Septuagenario A.D. VII ID. NOV. ANNO MCMLIII a Collegis Discipulis Amicis Dictata.* Copenhagen: Einar Munksgaard, 1953. Pp. 152–62.

JERVELL, JACOB. "Jesu blods aker. Matt. 27, 3–10." *Norsk Teologisk Tidsskrift* 69 (1968): 158–62. *NT Abstracts* 13:574.

KLAUSNER, JOSEPH. *Jesus of Nazareth: His Life, Times, and Teaching.* Tr. by Herbert Danby. New York: Macmillan, 1925 (paperback, Boston: Beacon Press). Pp. 324–29.

KNOX, A.D. "The Death of Judas." *The Journal of Theological Studies* 25 (1923–24): 289 f.

LAKE, KIRSOPP. "The Death of Judas." *The Beginnings of Christianity, Part I. The Acts of the Apostles.* Ed. by F.J. Foakes-Jackson and K. Lake. London: Macmillan. Vol. 5 (1933). Note IV, pp. 22–30.

LÜTHI, KURT. "Das Problem des Judas Iskariot—neu untersucht." *Evangelische Theologie* 16 (1956): 98–114.

PLATH, MARG. "Warum hat die urchristliche Gemeinde auf die Überlieferung der Judaserzählung Wert gelegt?" *Zeitschrift für die neutestamentliche Wissenschaft* 17 (1916): 178–88.

PREISKER, HERBERT. "Der Verrat des Judas und das Abendmahl." *Zeitschrift für die neutestamentliche Wissenschaft* 41 (1942): 151–55.

SCHLÄGER, G. "Die Ungeschichtlichkeit des Verräters Judas." *Zeitschrift für die neutestamentliche Wissenschaft* 15 (1914): 50–59.

SPITERI, A. *Die Frage der Judaskommunion neu untersucht.* Theologische Studien der Österreichischen Leo-Gesellschaft, 23. Vienna, 1918.

TORREY, CHARLES C. "The Name 'Iscariot.'" *Harvard Theological Review* 36 (1943): 51–62.

WRIGHT, A. "Was Judas Iscariot 'the first of the Twelve'?" *Interpreter* 13 (1916): 18–25.

SMART, JAMES D. *The Interpretation of Scripture.* Philadelphia: Westminster, 1961. Pp. 93–133.

FARRER, AUSTIN. "Important Hypotheses Reconsidered: VIII. Typology." *Expository Times* 67 (1955–56): 228–31. Reply by E. L. Wenger, *ibid.* 68 (1956–57): 222 f.

LAMPE, G. W. H., and K. J. WOOLLCOMBE. *Essays on Typology.* Studies in Biblical Theology, 22. London: SCM, 1957.

GOPPELT, LEONHARD. *Typos: Die typologische Deutung des Alten Testaments im Neuen.* Beiträge zur Förderung christlicher Theologie, 2. Reihe, 43. Gütersloh: Bertelsmann, 1939. Reprinted, Darmstadt: Wissenschaftliche Buchgesellschaft, 1969.

DANIÉLOU, JEAN. *From Shadows to Reality: Studies in the Biblical Typology of the Fathers.* London: Burns & Oates, 1960.

VON RAD, GERHARD. *Old Testament Theology.* Tr. by D. M. G. Stalker. New York: Harper & Row. Vol. 2 (1965), pp. 357–87.

WESTERMANN, CLAUS (ed.). *Essays on Old Testament Hermeneutics.* Richmond: John Knox, 1963.

ANDERSON, BERNHARD W. (ed.). *The Old Testament and the Christian Faith.* New York: Harper & Row, 1963.

Facet Books Already Published

Biblical Series:

1. *The Significance of the Bible for the Church*
   by Anders Nygren (translated by Carl Rasmussen). 1963
2. *The Sermon on the Mount*
   by Joachim Jeremias (translated by Norman Perrin). 1963
3. *The Old Testament in the New*
   by C. H. Dodd. 1963
4. *The Literary Impact of the Authorized Version*
   by C. S. Lewis. 1963
5. *The Meaning of Hope*
   by C. F. D. Moule. 1963
6. *Biblical Problems and Biblical Preaching*
   by C. K. Barrett. 1964
7. *The Genesis Accounts of Creation*
   by Claus Westermann (translated by Norman E. Wagner). 1964
8. *The Lord's Prayer*
   by Joachim Jeremias (translated by John Reumann). 1964

9. *Only to the House of Israel? Jesus and the Non-Jews*
   by T. W. Manson. 1964
10. *Jesus and the Wilderness Community at Qumran*
    by Ethelbert Stauffer (translated by Hans Spalteholz). 1964
11. *Corporate Personality in Ancient Israel*
    by H. Wheeler Robinson. 1964
12. *The Sacrifice of Christ*
    by C. F. D. Moule. 1964
13. *The Problem of the Historical Jesus*
    by Joachim Jeremias (translated by Norman Perrin). 1964
14. *A Primer of Old Testament Text Criticism*
    by D. R. Ap-Thomas. 1966
15. *The Bible and the Role of Women*
    by Krister Stendahl (translated by Emilie T. Sander). 1966
16. *Introduction to Pharisaism*
    by W. D. Davies. 1967
17. *Man and Nature in the New Testament*
    by C. F. D. Moule. 1967
18. *The Lord's Supper According to the New Testament*
    by Eduard Schweizer (translated by James M. Davis). 1967
19. *The Psalms: A Form-Critical Introduction*
    by Hermann Gunkel (translated by Thomas M. Horner). 1967
20. *The Spirit-Paraclete in the Fourth Gospel*
    by Hans Windisch (translated by James W. Cox). 1968
21. *The Semitic Background of the Term "Mystery" in the New Testament*
    by Raymond E. Brown, S.S. 1968
22. *The Beginnings of Christology: A Study in Its Problems*
    by Willi Marxsen (translated by Paul J. Achtemeier). 1969
23. *The Theology of the Book of Ruth*
    by Ronald M. Hals. 1969
24. *Luke the Historian in Recent Study*
    by C. K. Barrett. 1970
25. *The Lord's Supper as a Christological Problem*
    by Willi Marxsen (translated by Lorenz Nieting). 1970
26. *The "I Am" of the Fourth Gospel*
    by Philip B. Harner. 1970
27. *The Gospels and Contemporary Biographies in the Greco-Roman World*
    by Clyde Weber Votaw. 1970
28. *Was Jesus a Revolutionist?*
    by Martin Hengel (translated by William Klassen). 1971
29. *Iscariot*
    by Bertil Gärtner (translated by Victor I. Gruhn). 1971